# The Archaeology of
# New Testament Cities
# in Western Asia Minor

# The Archaeology of
# New Testament Cities
# in Western Asia Minor

Edwin M. Yamauchi

Pickering & Inglis
LONDON · GLASGOW

This edition 1980

ISBN 0 7208 0482 5
Cat. No. 01/0133

This edition is issued by
special arrangement with
Baker Book House
the American publishers

Printed in the United States of America for
PICKERING & INGLIS LTD., 26 Bothwell Street, Glasgow G2 6PA

To
**W. Harold Mare and Donald W. Burdick**
Colleagues in the Near East Archaeological Society

# ABBREVIATIONS

| | |
|---|---|
| *AJA* | *American Journal of Archaeology* |
| *Arch* | *Archaeology* |
| *AS* | *Anatolian Studies* |
| *BA* | *Biblical Archaeologist* |
| *Beiblatt* | *Jahreshefte des Österreichischen Archäologischen Instituts in Wien, Beiblatt* |
| *BH* | *Buried History* |
| *Hauptblatt* | *Jahreshefte des Österreichischen Archäologischen Instituts in Wien, Hauptblatt* |
| *IDBS* | *Interpreter's Dictionary of the Bible, Supplementary Volume* |
| *IM* | *Istanbuler Mitteilungen Deutsches Archäologisches Institut* |
| *NEASB* | *Near East Archaeological Society Bulletin* |
| *TB* | *Tyndale Bulletin* |

# FIGURES

## *Figure 1*

# ASIA MINOR

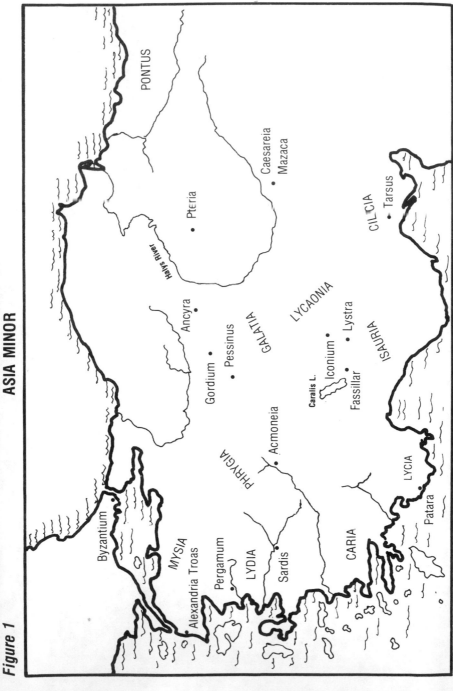

PONTUS

Halys River

Pteria •

Caesareia
Mazaca •

CILICIA

Tarsus •

Ancyra •

Gordium •

Pessinus •

GALATIA

LYCAONIA

Caralis L.

Iconium •

Lystra •

ISAURIA

Fassillar •

Acmoneia •

PHRYGIA

Byzantium •

MYSIA

Alexandria Troas •

Pergamum •

LYDIA

Sardis •

LYCIA

CARIA

Patara •

After Barbara Levick, *Roman Colonies in Southeast Asia Minor* (Oxford: Oxford
University Press, 1967)

# FOREWORD

Interpretation of the New Testament often suffers because of a lack of a good foundation of historical knowledge. Many twentieth-century Bible expositors are oblivious to the positive contribution of a century-and-a-half of scholarly endeavor in the field of history and approach the New Testament writings as though they had been written within the past few decades. Other Bible students, more academically oriented, are at least indirectly aware of the great work that has been done in the study of antiquity; but, rather than devoting their energies to the study of the New Testament documents themselves in the context of the history and literature of the Graeco-Roman world, they tend to focus on what other scholars are saying *about* the New Testament. In the former case, the result is unhistorical and idiosyncratic exegesis; in the latter, unsubstantial and often even absurd speculations. In either case, the Scripture is dishonored.

The work of Professor Yamauchi has always been a healthy corrective to these unhistorical approaches. Whether dealing with the literary and historical problems of the Book of Daniel (the subject of his earliest book) or the much-debated subject of the origins of Gnosticism (the subject of an important recent study), his views have always been rooted firmly in the hard data of historical research. In the present work he turns his attention to the archaeological background of the early Christian communities of western Asia Minor, and, in so doing, provides the student of the New Testament with a much needed aid.

This is a book which has cried out for a writer for many years, for no one since Sir William M. Ramsay at the turn of the century has brought together in such a fashion all of the material which has resulted from archaeological research into the life and times of the cities connected with the mission of Saint Paul and the Book of Revelation. True, there have been numerous essays and articles dedicated to the subject in recent years—the important work

of Colin J. Hemer is of special note—but there has been
no comprehensive study. Although he has not attempted
to be exhaustive, Yamauchi has written a fairly complete
account of the research related to these New Testament
cities, and thus he has done a great service for the scholarly community.

I have often mentioned the need for a book such as this
one, and have even thought of trying to do it myself. But
it is definitely for the best that the need has been met by
one who is much more deeply involved in the study of the
ancient world than I or others have been.

I am sure that *The Archaeology of New Testament Cities in
Western Asia Minor* will prove to be as interesting and as
helpful to others as it has proved to be to me. Every student of the letters of Paul, the Acts of the Apostles, and
the Book of Revelation will find much of value, as will
any brave travelers to Turkey who seek to retrace the
footsteps of Saint Paul. This is a book to which I will
surely be referring in my own studies in the future. It is
with a great deal of pleasure, therefore, that I commend
this work to all who love the Scriptures and who desire to
be faithful interpreters of them to others.

W. Ward Gasque
President
New College Berkeley

# PREFACE

Stimulated by a visit to western Turkey in 1974, I have sought to investigate the status of the archaeological information which we now have about key cities of western Asia Minor during the early Roman Empire. In this book I discuss the history and the monuments of certain key cities in a general north-to-south direction (see figure 2 for a map of western Asia Minor): (1) Assos, (2) Pergamum, (3) Thyateira, (4) Smyrna, (5) Sardis, (6) Philadelphia, (7) Ephesus, (8) Miletus, (9) Didyma, (10) Laodicea, (11) Hierapolis, and (12) Colossae.

These cities include the "Seven Cities" addressed in Revelation 2 and 3 (nos. 2, 3, 4, 5, 6, 7, 10), and also cities to which Paul sent letters (nos. 7, 10, 12). All except Didyma are mentioned in the New Testament. As commentators and other writers, most notably C. J. Hemer, have discussed the specific implications of the New Testament references to these cities, I have sought to present a broader historical perspective.

I have visited all of the cities with the exception of Thyateira and Philadelphia. With the exception of the photos of Colossae, which were taken by W. Harold Mare, all the photos were made from slides which I took in 1974. I am greatly indebted to Jerry Coltharp of the Audio-Visual Service of Miami University for his considerable efforts in preparing the maps and figures.

The publishers are to be commended for their interest in sponsoring this series in archaeology, and in reprinting the still valuable works of Sir William M. Ramsay.

I am especially indebted to W. Harold Mare, president of the Near East Archaeological Society, and to Donald W. Burdick, editor of the *Near East Archaeological Society Bulletin,* for permission to use materials from my article, "Recent Archaeological Work in the New Testament Cities of Western Anatolia," which appeared in numbers 13 and 14 of the *Bulletin.* With gratitude for their encouragement and fellowship in the gospel, I dedicate this book to them.

Finally, I would like to thank my son Brian, who used his computer skills to help me compile the indexes.

# CONTENTS

## Figure 2     WESTERN ASIA MINOR

# INTRODUCTION

## Asia

The modern country of Turkey is named after the nomadic Turks from Central Asia (Turkestan), whom the Arabs first employed as palace guards under the Abbassid ruler Al-Mutasim (833–42).[1] The Turks defeated the Byzantine emperor at the decisive battle of Manzikert near Lake Van in 1071, and gradually overran the entire Middle East, capturing Constantinople (Istanbul) in 1453.

The peninsula was called Anatolia (Turkish, *Anadolu*) by the Turks. We do not know when the name *Asia Minor* was first used but it was not prior to Orosius (5th century A.D.).[2] The word *Asia* may go back to the Hittite name *Assuwa*.[3] In the New Testament the word *Asia* usually refers to the Roman province which occupied the western part of Anatolia, and included the former territories of Caria, Ionia, and Lydia. In Acts 16:6 Paul was forbidden by the Holy Spirit to preach in Asia. Later, when he preached in Ephesus, all that dwelt in Asia heard the gospel (Acts 19:10). The word *Asia* is also used in the broader sense of Asia Minor, as in Acts 27:2.

## Historical Survey

Western Anatolia, which was on the fringes of the Hittite Empire, was subject to raids by the Mycenaean Greeks in the 13th century B.C., most notably in the famed siege

---

1. On the general subject of Turkey, see J. C. Dewdney, *Turkey* (New York: F. Praeger, 1971).
2. John A. Cramer, *A Geographical and Historical Description of Asia Minor* (Amsterdam: A. M. Hakkert, 1971 reprint of the 1832 edition), p. 3.
3. D. L. Page, *History and the Homeric Iliad* (Berkeley: University of California Press, 1959), p. 104: "We have securely placed the kingdom of *Assuwa* in a region which was known to the Greeks as *Asia:* Asia is a name earliest associated with the district of the River Caÿster and, not far north of it, the territory of Sardis. The greatest and strictest of Hittitologists admits that Hittite *Assuwa* and Greek *Asia* may well be the same word."

of Troy immortalized by Homer's *Iliad*.[4] Archaeology has confirmed the Greek tradition of the settlement of Ionia in western Asia Minor by Greek refugees fleeing from the Dorians in the 12th–11th centuries B.C.[5]

As the Aegean world emerged from the Dark Age, the Ionian cities led the way. Extensive evidence for the archaic period (8th–6th centuries B.C.) has been recovered at Smyrna.[6] During much of this time western Asia Minor was dominated by the powerful and fabulously wealthy kings of Sardis in Lydia.

The Persians under Cyrus captured Sardis and much of Ionia in 547/546 B.C. After failing in an abortive revolt in 499 to 494 B.C., the Ionians were liberated from the Persians by Alexander the Great.[7]

After Alexander's death various successors, including Lysimachus of Thrace and Seleucid rulers, fought each other for control of Asia Minor. The entire area in western Asia Minor enjoyed prosperity under the Attalid rulers of Pergamum. The last of the Pergamene kings, who was without an heir, bequeathed his kingdom to the Romans in 133 B.C. They reorganized his territories as the province of Asia.[8]

In 88 B.C. the rapacity of Roman businessmen and tax-collectors provoked the rebellion of Mithradates, the king of Pontus in northern Anatolia.[9] Mithradates ordered the killing of eighty thousand Italians resident in Asia. He is

---

4. E. Yamauchi, "Homer, History and Archaeology," *NEASB* 3 (1973): 21–42.

5. J. M. Cook, *The Greeks in Ionia and the East* (New York: F. Praeger, 1963).

6. J. M. Cook, "Old Smyrna, 1948–51," *Annual of the British School at Athens* 53–54 (1958–59): 1–34.

7. Chester G. Starr, "Greeks and Persians in the Fourth Century B.C.," *Iranica Antiqua* 11 (1975): 39–99.

8. A. N. Sherwin-White, "Roman Involvement in Anatolia, 167–88 B.C.," *Journal of Roman Studies* 67 (1977): 62–75.

9. A. Duggan, *He Died Old: Mithradates Eupator, King of Pontus* (London: Faber & Faber, 1958). M. J. Mellink, "Archaeology in Asia Minor," *AJA* 81 (1977): 308, reports: "A remarkable new epigraphic discovery was made in the church of St. John (at Ephesus).... The block has a 153-

even said to have ordered molten gold poured down the throat of one Roman. The Romans sent Sulla (88–85 B.C.) and then Lucullus and Pompey (74–63 B.C.) to subdue this dangerous foe.

In the period of the Roman Empire the key cities of Asia vied with each other to demonstrate their support for the emperors, beginning with Augustus.[10] On the occasion of his birthday in 9 B.C., the *Koinon* (Provincial Assembly) of Asia issued a flattering proclamation hailing the emperor as the "divine Caesar" and as Savior *(Sōtēr)*.[11] Much of what the excavators have recovered comes either from what the emperors donated, or from structures dedicated to the emperors.[12] G. M. A. Hanfmann observes:

> For these splendid cities of the Roman province of Asia, for Ephesus, Sardis, Miletus, and Pergamon, there began with the emperor Augustus an era of reconstruction and prosperity which continued to gain momentum through the first and second centuries A.D. until invasions of the Goths, Sassanian Persians, and Palmyrenes, after the middle of the third century broke the golden age of Roman peace.[13]

So thoroughgoing was the rebuilding of the Asian cities

---

line inscription dated July 8, A.D. 62, apparently containing an Asiatic tax and customs regulation."

10. For a general treatment of the relations between Augustus and the East, see G. W. Bowersock, *Augustus and the Greek World* (Oxford: Clarendon Press, 1965).

11. F. C. Grant, ed., *Ancient Roman Religion* (New York: Liberal Arts, 1957), pp. 173–74; Fergus Millar, *The Emperor in the Roman World* (London: Duckworth, 1977), p. 386.

12. Most Greek and Latin inscriptions relating to the emperors of the 1st century may be found in: *Documents Illustrating the Reigns of Augustus and Tiberius,* ed. V. Ehrenberg and A. H. M. Jones, 2nd ed. (Oxford: Clarendon Press, 1976); *Documents Illustrating the Principates of Gaius, Claudius and Nero,* ed. E. M. Smallwood (Cambridge: Cambridge University Press, 1967); *Select Documents of the Principates of the Flavian Emperors,* ed. M. McCrum and A. G. Woodhead, 2nd ed. (Cambridge: Cambridge University Press, 1966); *Documents Illustrating the Principates of Nerva, Trajan and Hadrian,* ed. E. M. Smallwood (Cambridge: Cambridge University Press, 1966).

13. G. M. A. Hanfmann, *From Croesus to Constantine* (Ann Arbor: University of Michigan Press, 1975), p. 42.

under the emperors that Henri Metzger comments: "Generally speaking, western and southern Anatolia were so thoroughly romanised that there is no local feeling to be detected under the buildings of the main Roman period."[14]

## Ramsay's Contributions

The greatest figure in the archaeology of Roman Asia Minor was Sir William Mitchell Ramsay (d. 1939). When he first set foot in Turkey in 1880, Ramsay was committed to the then dominant views of the Tübingen School.[15] But the results of his own researches in Asia Minor convinced him of the essential trustworthiness of the New Testament.[16] Ramsay effectively challenged the radical Tübingen School's dismissal of the Acts of the Apostles as a late and unreliable composition.[17]

In the years since Ramsay's death many of the major positions which he advocated have been accepted and reinforced by subsequent discoveries. It was Ramsay who argued for the southern or political designation of Galatia as opposed to the northern or ethnic explanation of the term as maintained by J. B. Lightfoot.[18] The lasting value

---

14. Henri Metzger, *Anatolia II* (London: Cresset, 1969), p. 191.

15. W. M. Ramsay, "Explorations of Asia Minor as Bearing on the Historical Trustworthiness of the New Testament," *The Victoria Institute's Transactions* (1907): 204–05.

16. W. M. Ramsay, *The Bearing of Recent Discovery on the Trustworthiness of the New Testament* (London: Hodder & Stoughton, 1915), Colin J. Hemer, "Luke the Historian," *Bulletin of the John Rylands Library* 60 (1977): 36–37; idem, "The Later Ramsay, A Supplementary Bibliography," *TB* 22 (1971): 119–24.

17. E. M. Yamauchi, *The Stones and the Scriptures* (Philadelphia: J. B. Lippincott, 1972), pp. 92–96; W. W. Gasque, *Sir William M. Ramsay* (Grand Rapids: Baker, 1966); idem, "The Historical Value of the Book of Acts," *Theologische Zeitschrift* 28 (1972): 177–96; idem, *A History of the Criticism of the Acts of the Apostles* (Grand Rapids: Wm. B. Eerdmans, 1975).

18. D. Guthrie, *New Testament Introduction: The Pauline Epistles*, 2nd ed. (Chicago: Inter-Varsity, 1963), pp. 72–79.

of Ramsay's contributions is attested by the reprinting of many of his books.[19]

A proper appreciation of Ramsay's contributions must avoid the extremes of simply ignoring him (as liberal scholars have sometimes done), or of blindly accepting his reprinted works (as conservative scholars have sometimes done). Work has continued apace in the archaeology of Asia Minor, requiring the rejection or modification of some of Ramsay's opinions.[20]

---

19. Fourteen of his books have been reprinted, ten of them by Baker; see Gasque, *Sir William M. Ramsay*, pp. 86–87. Since Gasque wrote in 1966, the following have been reprinted: *The Social Basis of Roman Power in Asia Minor* (Amsterdam: A. M. Hakkert, 1967); *Asianic Elements in Greek Civilization* (New York: AMS, 1969); *The Cities and Bishoprics of Phrygia* (New York: Arno, 1975).

20. E. M. Yamauchi, "Ramsay's Views on Archaeology in Asia Minor Reviewed," *The New Testament Student* V, ed. John Skilton (Philadelphia: Presbyterian & Reformed, forthcoming).

# 1

## ASSOS

### Location

According to Strabo (XIII.1, 57, and 66) Assos was "strong and well fortified . . . [with] a harbor formed by a great mole . . . a notable city." The port city of Assos is located on a scenic site bordering the Adramyttium Gulf just north of the island of Lesbos on the south coast of the region known as the Troad.[1]

Farther north, guarding the Hellespont (the Dardanelles), was the legendary city of Homer's Troy, which Heinrich Schliemann began excavating in 1870.[2] Some 10 miles south of ancient Troy lay the Hellenistic-Roman port of Alexandria Troas, a key city in New Testament times (Acts 16:8, 11; 20:5-6; 2 Cor. 2:12; 2 Tim. 4:13).[3]

On his second missionary journey Paul was forbidden by the Holy Spirit to preach the word in Asia and to go into

---

1. On the general subject of the Troad, see J. M. Cook, *The Troad* (London: Oxford University Press, 1973).
2. See E. M. Yamauchi, "Homer, History, and Archaeology," *NEASB* 3 (1973): 21–42.
3. See C. J. Hemer, "Alexandria Troas," *TB* 26 (1975): 79–112.

Bithynia. After traversing the region of Mysia he reached
Troas (Acts 16:6–8). W. P. Bowers has suggested that even
before Paul had the so-called Macedonian vision (Acts
16:9) in Troas, he may have planned to travel westward.

> The nature of the routes available to him for that journey
> suggests strongly that his journey to Troas was not that of a
> bewildered man groping for a point from which new op-
> tions could be considered, but that of a man already with a
> specific destination in mind. The geographical considera-
> tions make the journey to Troas most readily explicable as
> an intended first stage of a journey to Macedonia (if not
> also beyond).[4]

In this view, the vision of the Macedonian stranger simply
reinforced Paul's own resolve.

Alexandria Troas, which was a key city, has never been
excavated. There are a few remains visible including sections of the city wall and ruins of baths built by Herodes
Atticus, a famous rhetorician of the 2nd century A.D. The
site of the ancient harbor is now a lagoon.[5]

## New Testament References

In the final stages of the third missionary journey, after
spending seven days in Alexandria Troas, Paul chose to go
to Assos by land while his friends continued on board the
ship (Acts 20:6, 13–14). This was a distance of about 20
miles.[6]

It is possible that Paul wanted to be by himself as he
contemplated the probability that he would not see his
beloved friends in Asia any more (Acts 20:38). C. J. Hemer
has suggested that Paul may have lingered at Troas to
instruct the believers there, and then have left by the
swifter land route, perhaps on horseback, to get to Assos.[7]

---

4. W. P. Bowers, "Paul's Route Through Mysia," *Journal of Theological
Studies* 30 (1979): 511.

5. For photos and a description of the ruins of Troas, see D. W. Burdick, "With Paul in the Troad," *NEASB* 12 (1978): 50–53, 64–65. In
what follows I am greatly indebted to Professor Burdick's article.

6. H. V. Morton, *In the Steps of St. Paul* (London: Rich & Cowan, 1936),
p. 152.

7. Hemer, "Alexandria Troas," p. 105.

D. W. Burdick suggests that Paul may have wished to instruct the believers on the way to Assos.[8]

## Historical Background

Assos was founded by Aeolian immigrants from northern Greece in the early first millennium B.C. By 600 B.C. Assos had become the most important city of the Troad with a population of about twelve to fifteen thousand, according to J. T. Clarke.[9]  ·

In the 6th century B.C. Assos came under the domination of Lydia. After falling to the Persians when Cyrus conquered Sardis in 546 B.C., Assos regained its freedom with the Greek victory over the Persians at Mycale in 479. On the basis of the Athenian tribute lists, J. M. Cook estimates that the population of Assos in the 5th century had fallen to four thousand.[10]

In the 4th century B.C., Hermeias, a former slave who had studied under Plato, became the tyrant of Assos. When Speusippus succeeded Plato as the head of the Academy at the latter's death in 347, the disappointed Aristotle accepted the invitation of his friend and came to the court at Assos. He married the niece of Hermeias, Pythias. During his stay at Assos, Aristotle began work on his important treatise on *Politics*.[11] Aristotle then moved to Mitylene on the nearby island of Lesbos in 343 before going on to the Macedonian court to serve as the tutor of the young Alexander.

In 342 B.C. a Greek general serving the Persian king, Artaxerxes III (Ochus), seized Hermeias because he was an ally of Philip of Macedon. Hermeias was crucified by

8. Burdick, "With Paul in the Troad," p. 42.

9. J. T. Clarke, *Report on the Investigations at Assos, 1881* (Boston: A. Williams and Co., 1882), p. 77; and idem, *Report on the Investigations at Assos, 1882, 1883* (New York: Macmillan, 1898), p. 42, cited by Burdick, "With Paul in the Troad," pp. 54–55.

10. Cook, *The Troad*, p. 383.

11. H. Bengtson et al., *The Greeks and the Persians* (London: Weidenfeld & Nicolson, 1970), p. 261.

the Persian king. Aristotle composed a poem in his honor and set up his statue at Delphi.[12]

Cleanthes, the successor of Zeno as the head of the Stoics in Athens, was born in Assos in about 331 B.C. It was possibly from Cleanthes's "Hymn to Zeus" that Paul quoted the phrase, "For we are also his offspring," in his famous sermon on the Areopagus (Acts 17:28).[13]

**I.1** The well-preserved main gate.

## Excavations

Assos was excavated between 1881 and 1883 by Joseph T. Clarke and Francis H. Bacon. This was noteworthy as the first expedition sponsored by the newly established Archaeological Institute of America.

In recently published excerpts from the journals of Francis H. Bacon, we find the following complaint penned on September 6, 1881:

> It makes ones [sic] blood boil to think how this grand old city has been devastated within the last fifty years! The Turkish government has been carting away cut stones, and

12. *Cambridge Ancient History* IV: *Macedon 401–301 B.C.*, ed. J. B. Bury et al. (Cambridge: Cambridge University Press, 1927), pp. 23, 251, 334.

13. F. W. Farrar, *The Life and Work of St. Paul*, excursus III, "The Classic Quotations and Allusions of St. Paul" (London: Cassell & Co., 1903), pp. 696ff. The phrase also appears in Epimenides, *On Oracles,* and the "Hymn to Zeus" by Callimachus.

**I.2** Interior view of the main gate's tower.

every little village in the neighborhood comes here for
building material. Many a stone which might be the key of
our present problems has probably been carried off in this
manner.[14]

Some of the stone blocks from the theater were carted
away by the Turkish government in 1864 for the construction of new docks at Constantinople.

### The Monuments

The city walls, which were erected in the 4th century
B.C., are still in a marvelous state of preservation. Ac-

---

14. "The Assos Journals of Francis H. Bacon," ed. L. O. K. Congdon,
*Arch* 27.2 (1974): 90.

cording to E. Akurgal, "These walls are the most complete fortifications in the Greek world."[15] The north tower of the main gateway still stands to almost 50 feet (see photos I.1 and 2). The slits in this tower were used for bolt-projecting catapults.[16]

On top of the 700-foot-high acropolis stood the impressive temple of Athena. Fragments of the Ionic frieze of the temple are preserved in the Istanbul Museum, the Louvre, and the Boston Museum of Fine Arts.[17]

The trapezoidal agora was flanked by a North Stoa (see photo I.4), 115 meters (380 feet) long, in the direction of the acropolis, and a South Stoa, somewhat shorter, in the seaward direction.[18] The holes which are visible in the photo originally held wooden beams which supported the second floor. The South Stoa was a three-storied structure with thirteen shops on the middle floor and bathrooms on the lowest floor. An air space between these two floors kept the building cool in the summer and warm in the winter.

To the east of the North Stoa was the *bouleutērion* or council chamber. Between the Stoa and the council chamber was the *bēma* or speaker's rostrum. The mixture of Doric and Ionic styles in these structures reflects the period of Pergamene influence (241–133 B.C.).

The South Stoa overlooked the theater, where spectators would have had a clear view of the harbor below (see photo I.5). The ruins of the theater were still well preserved when Prokesch von Osten of Austria visited the site

---

15. E. Akurgal, *Ancient Civilizations and Ruins of Turkey*, 2nd ed. (Istanbul: Mobil Oil Türk A.S., 1970), p. 64; cf. R. Scranton, "Greek Arts in Greek Defenses," *Arch* 3.1 (1950): 4–12; F. E. Winger, "Notes on Military Architecture in the Termessos Region," *AJA* 70 (1966): 127–37.

16. Cf. C. W. Soedel and V. Foley, "Ancient Catapults," *Scientific American* 240.3 (1979): 150–60.

17. See photos 6–10 in Burdick, "With Paul in the Troad," pp. 58–60.

18. R. E. Wycherley, *How the Greeks Built Cities* (London: Macmillan, 1962), pp. 78–79, 116. For an idea of the appearance of such a stoa or colonnaded porch one can view the reconstructed stoa of Attalus II in Athens. See *The Stoa of Attalos II in Athens* (Princeton: American School of Classical Studies at Athens, 1959).

**I.3**
Details of the fortifications, which are among the best-preserved of Hellenistic structures (4th century B.C.).

**I.4**
Remains of the North Stoa with the acropolis in the background.

in 1826, but they have been plundered since then.[19] At that time there were still forty rows of seats visible. According to the American excavators, two blind corridors led to a cistern and to latrines. The Italian investigator, Bernardi Ferrero, however, could not find any evidence to support these interpretations.[20]

## The Imperial Cult

With the death of the last Pergamene king in 133 B.C. Assos together with the rest of western Asia Minor fell under the aegis of Rome. Inscriptions from Assos reveal the presence of many resident Romans.[21] Other inscriptions reveal that the city of Assos assiduously cultivated the favor of the Roman emperors. A stoa near the gymnasium bore the following inscription:

> The priest of the god Caesar Augustus, himself likewise hereditary king, priest of Zeus Homonoos, and gymnasiarch, Quintus Lollius Philetairos, has dedicated the Stoa to the god Caesar Augustus and the people.[22]

The donor's wife also dedicated a bath to the empress:

> Lollia Antiochis, wife of Quintus Lollius Philetairos, first of women, who was queen in accordance with ancestral customs, dedicated this Bath and its belongings to Julia Aphrodite [i.e., Livia] and the people [of Rome].[23]

Augustus had pinned his hopes for succession upon the sons of his daughter Julia and Marcus Agrippa—Gaius and Lucius. Numerous statues of these young grandsons of Augustus have been found in Asia Minor, including a

19. Daria de Bernardi Ferrero, *Teatri Classici in Asia Minore* III: *Città dalla Troade alla Pamfilia* (Rome: "L'Erma" di Bretschneider, 1970), pp. 37ff.

20. Ibid., p. 39.

21. T. R. S. Broughton, "Roman Asia," in *An Economic Survey of Ancient Rome*, ed. T. Frank (Baltimore: Johns Hopkins University Press, 1938), vol. IV, pp. 716–17, 881.

22. C. C. Vermeule, *Roman Imperial Art in Greece and Asia Minor* (Cambridge: Harvard University Press, 1968), p. 216.

23. Ibid., pp. 216, 457.

**1.5** The harbor where Paul rejoined Luke (Acts 20:13–14).

statue of Gaius at Assos.[24] Alas for Augustus's hopes, Lucius died in A.D. 2 and Gaius was fatally wounded in A.D. 4.

When Gaius Caligula became emperor (A.D. 37) five citizens from Assos went to Rome to sacrifice to the Capitoline Jupiter in the name of their city. An inscription records that a stoa was dedicated to the emperor Claudius (41–54). No further artifacts from the imperial period have been recovered until we come to the 3rd century A.D., from which we have a statue of Julia Domna, the wife of Septimius Severus (193–211).[25]

24. Ibid., pp. 179–80, 456.
25. Ibid., p. 457. For an extensive bibliography on the coins of Assos, see Bernardi Ferrero, *Teatri Classici*, p. 42.

*Figure 3*

## THE UPPER ACROPOLIS OF PERGAMUM

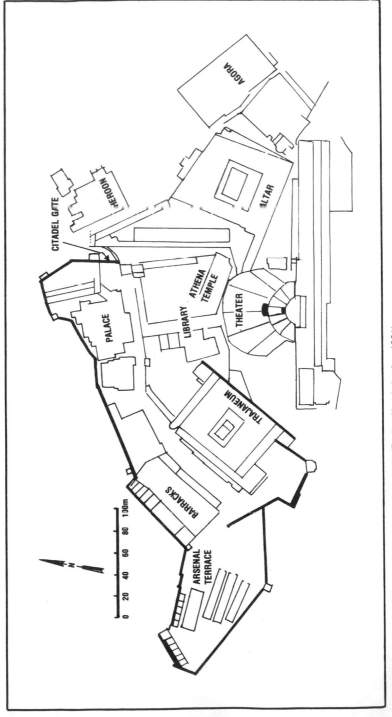

After Elizabeth Rhode, *Pergamon, Burgberg, und Altar* (Berlin: Henchelverlag, 1961)

# 2

## PERGAMUM

### Location

Pergamum is located 15 miles inland and 2 miles north of the Caicus River in southern Mysia (see figures 1 and 2). Its citadel was located on a hill which towers 900 feet above the plain (see photo II.1). M. J. Mellink has called it "easily the most spectacular city of Asia Minor."[1] W. M. Ramsay exclaimed:

> No city of the whole of Asia Minor—so far as I have seen, and there are few of any importance which I have not seen—possesses the same imposing and dominating aspect. It is the one city of the land which forced from me the exclamation "A royal city!"[2]

The upper acropolis (figure 3) was occupied by the palace, the library, the Athena temple, the Trajaneum, the barracks, and the arsenal terrace. At a level 80 feet lower was the site of the great Altar of Zeus. The theater was

---

1. M. J. Mellink, "Pergamum," *The Interpreter's Dictionary of the Bible,* ed. G. A. Buttrick et al. (Nashville: Abingdon, 1962), vol. III, p. 734.
2. W. M. Ramsay, *Letters to the Seven Churches of Asia* (Grand Rapids: Baker, 1979 reprint), p. 295.

II.1 The striking acropolis rises 900 feet above the plain.

placed on the steep southern slope with a magnificent view over the plain. Along the slopes to the northeast were the three major gymnasia. The healing shrine of the Asklepieion was located on the plain.

### New Testament References

Many commentators have linked the "throne of Satan" at Pergamum (Rev. 2:13) with the great Altar of Zeus.[3] Some have suggested a reference to the appearance of the city hill, while others have seen a reference to the cult of Asklepios.[4] The only other reference to Pergamum is in the introduction to the seven letters (Rev. 1:11).

---

3. Ibid., p. 43; David Magie, *Roman Rule in Asia Minor* (Princeton: Princeton University Press, 1950), vol. II, p. 771; Robert H. Mounce, *The Book of Revelation* (Grand Rapids: Wm. B. Eerdmans, 1977), p. 95. I have not seen Theodor Birt, "Der Thron des Satan: Ein Beitrag zur Erklärung des Altars von Pergamon," *Berliner Philologische Wochenschrift* 52 (1932): 1203–10.

4. Colin J. Hemer, "Unto the Angels of the Churches," *BH* 11 (1975): 73. Hemer has written a series of four excellent articles on the seven churches of Revelation in the popular journal, *Buried History* (hereafter *BH*), published by the Australian Institute of Archaeology: 11 (1975), 4–27, 56–83, 110–35, 164–90. In 1969 he wrote a dissertation at Manchester University titled, "A Study of the Letters to the Seven Churches of Asia with Special Reference to Their Local Background." A revised version is to be published in the New Testament Studies monograph series by Cambridge University Press.

## Historical Background

After the death of Alexander, Lysimachus gained control of the region around Pergamum. It was his rebellious treasurer, Philetaerus, who established the Pergamene dynasty of the Attalids in 283 B.C. Philetaerus dedicated the sanctuary to Athena and aspired to make the city the Athens of Asia Minor. The dynasty of the Pergamene kings ran as follows:[5]

| | |
|---|---|
| Philetaerus | 283–263 B.C. |
| Eumenes I | 263–241 |
| Attalus I | 241–197 |
| Eumenes II | 197–159 |
| Attalus II | 159–138 |
| Attalus III | 138–133 |

The first three kings had to fight the marauding Galatians. Attalus I set up statues of the defeated Galatian warriors killing themselves. In commemoration of Attalus I's victory over the Galatians Eumenes II erected the Altar of Zeus. He also built the city's library. Attalus II paid for a magnificent stoa, 116 meters (380 feet) long, in the agora at Athens. The modern replica of the stoa now serves as a museum.[6] The *heroon* set up outside the citadel gate (figure 3) served as a sanctuary in honor of the heroized kings.

## Excavations

In 1878, some eight years after Schliemann had initiated Aegean archaeology with his spectacular discoveries at Troy, other Germans, Carl Humann, Alexander Conze, and R. Bohn began to clear the upper city of Pergamum. Schliemann's assistant W. Dörpfeld, together with H.

---

5. See E. V. Hansen, *The Attalids of Pergamon* (Ithaca: Cornell University Press, 1947), pp. 237, 448. The gate to the sanctuary of Athena Polias has been restored in the Pergamum Museum in East Berlin. See also M. J. Price and B. L. Trell, *Coins and Their Cities* (Detroit: Wayne State University Press, 1977), p. 104.

6. H. A. Thompson, *The Stoa of Attalus at Athens* (Princeton: American School of Classical Studies, 1959); R. E. Wycherley, *How the Greeks Built Cities* (London: Macmillan, 1962), pp. 84, 116; Hansen, *Attalids of Pergamon*, p. 297.

Hepding and P. Schatzman, worked in the middle and
lower districts from 1900 to 1913. Between 1927 and 1935
Theodor Wiegand directed the excavations of the arsen-
als, the Red Basilica, and the Asklepieion.[7] Henri Metzger
comments:

> The excavations carried out at Pergamon by the Berlin
> Museum between 1878 and 1886, and by the German Ar-
> chaeological Institute in the inter-war period and again
> since 1951, have made it possible to follow the splendid
> development of a royal city which until the beginning of
> the third century (B.C.) was limited to the dimensions of a
> mere fortress, and then expanded on a succession of ter-
> races harmoniously grouped round a steeply raked theatre
> and a number of horizontal porticoes.[8]

After earlier work in the Asklepieion in the 1920s and
1930s, Erich Boehringer completed excavations there
between 1958 and 1963.[9] The latest efforts, resumed since
1971 under Oskar Ziegenaus and Wolfgang Radt, have
concentrated on the slopes just below the summit of the
acropolis.

Along the main street which curves up the acropolis, the
excavators have found that many new buildings replaced
earlier Hellenistic structures in the 1st century A.D., perhaps after an earthquake.[10] This was also the time when
the sewers and drains, which serviced the urinals and latrines in the area, were cleaned out.

The system of water supply and drainage at Pergamum
was impressively engineered. According to W. Tarn, "the
supply for the hill at Pergamum was forced up the last two

7. Ekrem Akurgal, *Ancient Civilizations and Ruins of Turkey* (Istanbul:
Mobil Oil Türk A.S., 1970), p. 7. This is easily the best guide to Greco-
Roman antiquities in Turkey. It may be ordered c/o The Public Affairs
Department of the publisher, P.K. 600, Istanbul. *Biblical Sites in Turkey*
by E. C. Blake and A. G. Edmonds (Istanbul: Redhouse Press, 1977) is
disappointingly brief and superficial.

8. Henri Metzger, *Anatolia II* (London: Cresset, 1969), p. 191.

9. Oskar Ziegenaus and Gioia de Luca, *Altertümer von Pergamon: Das
Asklepieion* I & II (Berlin: W. de Gruyter, 1968, 1975).

10. W. Radt, "Pergamon: Vorbericht über die Kampagne 1976," *Ar-
chäologischer Anzeiger des Jahrbuches des Deutschen Archäologischen Instituts*
(1977): 304–05.

miles through metal pipes under a pressure of 18 atmos-
pheres."[11] The excavators found that in the reign of
Claudius a new pipe for drinking water was installed in the
road just north of the recently discovered baths.

A well-preserved *odeion* or auditorium (see photo II.5)
has been uncovered, and its tiers of seats restored.[12] Also
restored next to the *odeion* is the "Marble Hall," which
served as a *heroon* or shrine to a departed hero. Nearby was
uncovered a food shop, where the remains of meals were
found in a pit.[13]

Salvage operations by the Turks in an area east of Pergamum which is to be flooded by the Kestel Dam have
recently brought to light the area in which the pottery
makers worked. The site, which was used from the Hellenistic to the Byzantine period, has yielded a "rich series
of relief bowls and moulds for friezes and medallions."[14]

## The Altar of Zeus

Carl Humann found that the Byzantines had reused
parts of the Altar of Zeus in their fortification walls in
about A.D. 1000. E. V. Hansen remarks: "The fact that
most of the heads of the gods are gone probably indicates
the zeal of the early Christians in destroying all evidence of
this, the most complete representation of the Greek pantheon."[15]

The word *altar* is somewhat misleading. The structure is
a monumental colonnaded court in the form of a horse-
shoe, 120 by 112 feet. The podium of the altar was nearly
18 feet high. The great frieze, which ran at the base of the

---

11. W. Tarn and G. T. Griffith, *Hellenistic Civilisation*, 3rd ed. (London:
Edward Arnold, 1952), p. 311. On Roman hydraulic engineering, see
Vitruvius, *The Ten Books on Architecture*, tr. M. H. Morgan (New York:
Dover, 1960 reprint of 1914 ed.), pp. 244–48.

12. W. Radt, "Pergamon: Vorbericht über die Kampagne 1977," *Ar-
chäologischer Anzeiger* (1978): 423–25.

13. Radt, "Pergamon: Vorbericht über die Kampagne 1976," pp.
313–14.

14. M. Mellink, "Archaeology in Asia Minor," *AJA* 83 (1979): 341.

15. Hansen, *Attalids of Pergamon*, p. 338.

structure for 446 feet, depicted a gigantomachy, that is, a battle of the gods and the giants. It was one of the greatest works of Hellenistic art.[16]

Following the evidence from coins, Otto Puchstein labored for twenty years to reassemble the marble fragments of the altar. He may have been misled by the numismatic evidence in some details.[17] Once assembled the altar was the centerpiece for the Pergamum Museum, which opened in 1930 as the world's first museum of architecture. The museum, which is now in East Berlin, ranks in size third after the British Museum and the Louvre. It houses among other monuments the restored Ishtar Gate of Nebuchadnezzar's Babylon. During World War II the altar was fortunately taken into a bombproof shelter as the building itself was heavily damaged during the Allied bombing raids.

At the site of Pergamum itself all that can be seen is the base of the altar (see photo II.2).

## The Library

The famous library, which was located on top of the acropolis, was second only to the library in Alexandria. When Ptolemy V refused to sell papyrus to Eumenes II, the Pergamenes treated sheep- and goatskins to produce parchment (Latin, *pergamentum*). The library is said to have held two hundred thousand volumes when Mark Antony offered it to Cleopatra.[18]

The large hall which served as a reading room measured 13.5 by 16 meters (44 by 52.5 feet). Holes in the walls indicate the location of bookshelves. It has been estimated that the main room could have held only 12,500 rolls, so the rest must have been stored elsewhere.[19]

---

16. T. B. L. Webster, *Hellenistic Poetry and Art* (New York: Barnes and Noble, 1964), pp. 189–91. The Altar of Zeus may have inspired the *Ara Pacis* ("Altar of Peace") of Augustus. See P. MacKendrick, *The Mute Stones Speak* (New York: St. Martin's Press, 1960), pp. 156–70.

17. Price and Trell, *Coins and Their Cities*, pp. 119, 122.

18. Hansen, *Attalids of Pergamon*, p. 274.

19. B. Götze, "Antike Bibliotheken," *Jahrbuch der Deutschen Archäologischen Instituts* 52 (1937): 230–37. Cf. R. Triomphe, "Sur le dispositif intérieur des bibliothèques antiques," *Revue archéologique* 2

II.2 The foundation of the great Altar of Zeus.

II.3
The steeply slanted theater (3rd century B.C.) could
accommodate ten thousand spectators.

## The Theater

Just south of the library and the temple of Athena is the steeply slanted theater, which could have accommodated ten thousand spectators (see photo II.3). The scene building is located 122 feet below the top row of seats. The audience could have promenaded to the theater in the shade of a 245-foot-long portico. The panorama from the theater is truly breathtaking.[20]

## The Gymnasia

The word *gymnasium* comes through Latin from the Greek word γυμνάσιον, the place where athletic exercises were practiced in the nude (γυμνός). In 1 Timothy 4:8 appears the word γυμνασία, which means "bodily exercises." The gymnasium was also a place where lectures were given. Socrates taught in the gymnasia. Plato established his school at the Academy and Aristotle at the Lyceum—both gymnasia. With the conquests of Alexander the gymnasia became the chief acculturating institution of Hellenism.[21]

In the Roman period the gymnasium served as the chief center of the educational and social life of the community. There were at least seven at Pergamum, three at Miletus and at Thyateira. At Dorylaeum there was even one for women.[22] G. M. A. Hanfmann summarizes the gym-

(1938): 248–51; C. Callmer, "Antike Bibliotheken," *Opuscula Archaeologica* 3 (1944): 145–93.

20. Daria de Bernardi Ferrero, *Teatri Classici in Asia Minore* III: *Città dalla Troade alla Pamfilia* (Rome: "L'Erma" di Bretschneider, 1970), pp. 23–33.

21. E. N. Gardiner, *Greek Athletics, Sports and Festivals* (London: Macmillan, 1910); J. Delorme, *Gymnasion* (Paris: E. de Boccard, 1960). On the Jews and Greek athletics, see H. A. Harris, *Greek Athletics and the Jews* (Cardiff: University of Wales Press, 1976); A. Kasher, "The Jewish Attitude to the Alexandrian Gymnasium in the First Century A.D.," *American Journal of Ancient History* 1 (1976): 148–61; M. Avi-Yonah, *Hellenism and the East* (Ann Arbor: University Microfilms, 1978), pp. 126–29. My student, Roger Chambers, has written a dissertation on this topic, "Greek Athletics and the Jews: 165 B.C.–A.D. 70" (Miami University, 1980).

22. Magie, *Roman Rule*, vol. I, p. 652.

nasium's importance: "With its multiple functions as civic center, club house, leisure area, school, and place of worship of emperors, the gymnasium now replaced the palace and the temple as the major concern of Asiatic cities."[23] The gymnasia of the Roman period differed from earlier Greek buildings. According to R. E. Wycherley, "In Roman times athletic establishments became infinitely more luxurious, though the old types too continued. In particular they were provided with elaborate hot baths."[24]

Both in Greek and in Roman society wealthy citizens were expected to share their wealth for civic purposes. (Consider, for example, the donation of Erastus, the treasurer of Corinth.[25]) For their donations they were honored with statues and inscriptions.

> The machinery of Greek city life was sustained by interaction between rich and poor: the rich were led by love of honor *(philotimia)* and fear of envy to be generous to their humbler fellow-citizens, while these in turn rewarded them with an elaborately graded range of distinctions.[26]

In addition to erecting buildings, sponsoring entertainments such as gladiatorial games, and so forth, the wealthy were expected to serve as *gymnasiarchai,* officials in charge of the gymnasia, and as *agōnothetai,* officials in charge of athletic festivals. The gymnasiarch was expected to furnish the oil for the exercisers. The *agōnothetēs* was expected to furnish not only the oil but prizes and refreshments.[27]

The three major gymnasia of Pergamum were placed on adjoining terraces: (1) the upper gymnasium for young men over twenty *(neoi),* (2) the middle gymnasium for

23. G. M. A. Hanfmann, *From Croesus to Constantine* (Ann Arbor: University of Michigan Press, 1975), p. 48.

24. Wycherley, *How the Greeks Built Cities,* p. 153. I have not seen F. K. Yegül, "The Bath-Gymnasium Complex in Asia Minor During the Imperial Roman Age" (Ph.D. dissertation, Harvard University, 1975).

25. E. M. Yamauchi, *The Stones and the Scriptures* (Philadelphia: J. B. Lippincott, 1972), p. 116.

26. C. P. Jones, *The Roman World of Dio Chrysostom* (Cambridge: Harvard University Press, 1978), p. 28.

27. Magie, *Roman Rule,* vol. I, pp. 652–54.

II.4 The middle of three gymnasia served adolescent youths.

II.5
An *odeion* (small auditorium) was discovered by German
excavators in 1974.

adolescents *(ephēboi)* (see photo II.4), and (3) the lower gymnasium for little boys *(paides)*. The middle terrace extends 500 by 118 feet. Access to it was through a well-preserved vaulted staircase, which is "one of the finest examples of its kind from the Greek period."[28] The two upper gymnasia attracted young men and ephebes from throughout the Pergamene kingdom. The lower gymnasium, which had no classrooms, was attended only by local boys.

After graduation from the ranks of the ephebes, the *neoi* continued their association as a corporate body. They had their own funds, their own assemblies, and their own officials.[29] Lists of promotions from the middle of the 2nd century B.C. suggest that the population of Pergamum was about 120,000.[30]

Discoveries of the German excavators since 1974 have included a complex of buildings with an *odeion* (small auditorium) (see photo II.5), a bath, and a palaestra (wrestling arena). This is interpreted as either a small gymnasium or a kind of school for athletics.[31]

## The Imperial Cult

Pergamum was one of the first Asian cities to welcome Rome as an ally. In 133 B.C. Attalus II bequeathed his kingdom to the Romans. Julius Caesar was honored here with a statue as early as 63 B.C. Though there is some doubt as to how long Pergamum remained the capital of the province before it yielded this title to Ephesus,[32] there is no question but that it remained the focal point of the worship of the Roman emperors. As Ramsay observed:

> Here was built the first Asian Temple of the divine Augustus, which for more than forty years was the one centre of the Imperial religion for the whole Province. A second

28. Hansen, *Attalids of Pergamon*, p. 254.
29. W. M. Ramsay, *The Cities and Bishoprics of Phrygia* (Oxford: Clarendon Press, 1895), vol. I, p. 111.
30. Hansen, *Attalids of Pergamon*, p. 392.
31. M. J. Mellink, "Archaeology in Asia Minor," *AJA* 80 (1976): 282.
32. Hemer, "Unto the Angels," p. 72.

Asian Temple had afterwards been built at Smyrna, and a third at Ephesus; but they were secondary to the original Augustan Temple at Pergamum.[33]

The Pergamenes honored Augustus on his birthday with a choir of forty singing hymns.[34] H. Ingholt has argued that the original of the famous Prima Porta statue of Augustus once stood on the so-called round monument in the court of the Temple of Athena.[35] He was the first in a long line of emperors down to Elagabalus to be honored with statues at Pergamum.[36]

The outstanding imperial sanctuary was the Trajaneum (figure 3), built by Hadrian in honor of his adoptive father and predecessor. The Trajaneum, 68 by 58 meters (223 by 190 feet), was built on the highest point of the acropolis, It was by far the most splendid monument erected to Trajan anywhere in Asia. The deified Trajan and Zeus Philios ("The Friendly") were honored with a new festival. Later the deified Hadrian was also worshiped here.[37] The earlier excavations recovered colossal marble heads of Trajan and of Hadrian which are now in the Berlin Museum. Recent work at restoration since 1974 has uncovered a left hand and shod foot which were probably once part of the colossal statue of Trajan or Hadrian.[38]

By the early third century under Caracalla Pergamum had been honored not only as δὶς νεωκόρος but as τρὶς νεωκόρος, that is, as "twice warden" and "thrice warden" of the emperor's temple. The term neōkoros, which literally means "temple sweeper," became an honorific title as at

---

33. Ramsay, *Letters to the Seven Churches*, p. 294. Cf. Price and Trell, *Coins and Their Cities*, p. 192.

34. Magie, *Roman Rule*, vol. I, p. 448.

35. H. Ingholt, "The Prima Porta Statue of Augustus," *Arch* 22 (1969): 176–87, 304–18.

36. C. C. Vermeule, *Roman Imperial Art in Greece and Asia Minor* (Cambridge: Harvard University Press, 1968), pp. 214, 229ff., 455–56.

37. Magie, *Roman Rule*, vol. I, p. 594; Akurgal, *Ancient Civilizations*, p. 82; Jones, *Roman World*, p. 117. For a numismatic view of the temple, see Price and Trell, *Coins and Their Cities*, p. 16.

38. M. J. Mellink, "Archaeology in Asia Minor," *AJA* 82 (1978): 330; Radt, "Pergamon: Vorbericht über die Kampagne 1977," p. 428.

Ephesus, where it was used in connection with the temple of Artemis (see p. 108).[39]

## Temples

One of the more important temples was that dedicated to Demeter and Persephone, which was located on the northern slopes of the acropolis (see photos II.6 and 7). A bank of steps may have served as a viewing stand for the mystery rites of Demeter, perhaps similar to those presented at Eleusis west of Athens.[40]

The largest structure still standing at Pergamum is the so-called Red Basilica (or Hall) at the base of the hill (see photo II.8). This was erected under Trajan or Hadrian as a temple to the Egyptian gods Serapis, Isis, and Harpocrates.[41] The building and its court are 100 by 200 meters (328 by 656 feet). The main building is flanked by two round towers which rise about 16 meters (52.5 feet) from the ground. D. Boyd makes the following suggestion about the sanctuary: "A hole in the base gave entry to a subterranean tunnel through which the priests may have entered the cult statue in order to speak in the god's person."[42] The building was converted to a church dedicated to St. John in the Byzantine era; the left round tower serves today as a mosque.[43]

The recent excavations east of the *odeion* have uncovered a "podium hall," 24 by 10 meters (78 by 33 feet), which seems to have been the sanctuary of either Mithras or Attis, though no inscriptions have yet been found to identify the cult securely.[44] The worshipers must have

39. Yamauchi, *The Stones and the Scriptures,* p. 119.

40. C. Kerényi, *Eleusis* (London: Routledge & Kegan Paul, 1967).

41. Akurgal, *Ancient Civilizations,* p. 103.

42. D. Boyd, "Pergamum," *IDBS,* p. 654. Compare the trickery of the quack Alexander, who úsed the windpipes of cranes to make it appear that a snake could speak (Lucian, *Satirical Sketches,* tr. Paul Turner [Harmondsworth: Penguin, 1961], p. 233).

43. R. Salditt-Trappmann, *Tempel der ägyptischen Götter in Griechenland und an der Westküste Kleinasiens* (Leiden: E. J. Brill, 1970), pp. 10ff.

44. W. Radt, "Pergamon, 1976," *AS* 27 (1977): 50–51; M. J. Mellink, "Archaeology in Asia Minor," *AJA* 81 (1977): 310–13.

**II.6** This temple to Demeter and Persephone was built in the 3rd century B.C.

**II.7** The large altar of the temple of Demeter and Persephone.

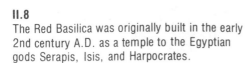

**II.8**
The Red Basilica was originally built in the early 2nd century A.D. as a temple to the Egyptian gods Serapis, Isis, and Harpocrates.

used the bench, 2 meters wide and 1 meter high, which ran
along the interior of the building for their cult meal. A pit
outside contained animal bones, possibly from the sanguinary rite called the *taurobolium* in which a bull was
slaughtered over an initiate.[45]

An altar and cult niche were also uncovered. On one
wall of the building was an orientalized male figure in
white robes over blue trousers, whose upper torso was unfortunately damaged. He stands in a grape arbor. In the
forecourt was a well which may have been used for ritual
lustrations. To the west of the room was found a herm of a
figure with a Phrygian cap, perhaps Mithras or Attis.[46]
The heyday of the building was in the 2nd and 3rd centuries A.D.

## The Asklepieion

The famed sanctuary of Asklepios, which was located
southeast of the acropolis, became the most important
healing center next to that of Epidaurus in Greece (see
photos II.9–11).[47] The cult of Asklepios was introduced
from Epidaurus to Pergamum in about 350 B.C. Both
archaeological and literary evidences indicate that the
sanctuary reached the peak of its popularity in the 2nd
century A.D.[48] The sanctuary is approached by a Sacred

---

45. Radt, "Pergamon: Vorbericht über die Kampagne 1977," pp.
418–19. On the cults of Mithras and of Isis, the *taurobolium,* and alleged
relations to Christianity, see M. J. Vermaseren, *Mithras, The Secret God*
(London: Chatto & Windus, 1963); R. Duthoy, *The Taurobolium* (Leiden: E. J. Brill, 1969); G. Wagner, *Pauline Baptism and the Pagan Mys-
teries* (Edinburgh: Oliver & Boyd, 1967); B. Metzger, *Historical and
Literary Studies* (Grand Rapids: Wm. B. Eerdmans, 1968), pp. 11ff.;
E. M. Yamauchi, "Easter—Myth, Hallucination, or History?" *Christianity Today* 18.12 (1974): 4–6.

46. Radt, "Pergamon: Vorbericht über die Kampagne 1976," p. 311.

47. E. J. and L. Edelstein, eds., *Asclepius* (Baltimore: Johns Hopkins
University Press, 1945); C. Kerényi, *Asklepios* (Princeton: Princeton
University Press, 1959); A. Charitonidou, "Epidaurus: The Sanctuary
of Asclepius," in *Temples and Sanctuaries of Ancient Greece,* ed. Evi Melas
(London: Thames and Hudson, 1973), pp. 89–99.

48. Ziegenaus and de Luca, *Altertümer von Pergamon,* vol. I, p. 10.

**II.9** The *Asklepieion*. One of the colonnaded stoas (porticos).

**II.10** The *Asklepieion*. A general view of the famed healing center, which reached the height of its popularity in the 2nd century A.D.

**II.11** The *Asklepieion*. One of the sacred pools used by the sick and diseased.

Way, 820 meters (2700 feet) in length. By 1968 the excavators had cleared a 140-meter (460-foot) section of the colonnaded Roman street.[49]

The Asklepieion covers an area 110 by 130 meters (361 by 426.5 feet), with stoas on three sides. One enters the precinct from the northeast.[50] In this corner is a room dedicated to Hadrian, which served as a small library. In the northwest corner is a relatively small theater which could have seated 3,500. In the southwest corner were located lavatories, one for men with forty decorated marble seats, and a smaller one for women with seventeen seats.

In the southeast corner stood a two-story cylindrical building 26.5 meters (87 feet) in diameter with six apses which served as a healing center. Next to it is the round temple of Asklepios built in about A.D. 145 on the model of the Pantheon. It had a dome 43.5 meters (143 feet) in diameter. Running northwest from the treatment center to the sacred pools is a tunnel 80 meters (262.5 feet) long. The sacred spring and the pools provided the water and the mud used for the treatments.

We get a vivid insight into the kinds of treatments which invalids underwent at Pergamum from the writings of the distinguished rhetorician and chronic invalid, Aelius Aristides. Aristides was born in A.D. 118 in Mysia. After studying at Smyrna, Pergamum, and Athens, he began a brilliant career. But persistent illnesses such as smallpox, respiratory problems, and intestinal ailments led him to seek relief for years upon end at shrines like the Pergamene Asklepieion.[51] He endured mudpacks and bloodletting, ran barefoot in the cold, bathed in swollen rivers,

---

49. O. Ziegenaus, "Pergamon, 1969," *AS* 20 (1970): 19; M. J. Mellink, "Archaeology in Asia Minor," *AJA* 74 (1970): 173.

50. Akurgal, *Ancient Civilizations*, p. 108.

51. C. A. Behr, *Aelius Aristides and the Sacred Tales* (Amsterdam: A. M. Hakkert, 1968), pp. 164–68.

and walked 50 miles in the broiling sun.[52] Like other patients he performed the rite of incubation:

> Men in their sickness came to the temples of Asclepius to perform the rite of incubation, which meant simply that they slept the night (or sometimes even the day) in the temple, in hopes that the God Asclepius would either miraculously cure their ailment, or appear to them (or their attendants) in a dream with a direct prescription by which they might cure it themselves, or at least send them a dream which contained the cure, although in a somewhat enigmatic form.[53]

Pergamum was the birthplace of Galen (b. A.D. 129), who was to be revered as one of the most illustrious physicians of the ancient world. After studying at Smyrna, Alexandria, and Corinth, Galen served as physician to the emperors Marcus Aurelius, Commodus, and Septimius Severus.

---

52. Ibid., pp. 37–39.
53. Ibid., p. 34.

# 3

## THYATEIRA

### Location

Thyateira, one of the seven cities of Revelation (Rev. 1:11; 2:18, 24), was located about 35 miles inland southeast of Pergamum. It was a Macedonian colony and in the Roman period was, as Pliny the Elder called it, *inhonora civitas* ("a city of no first-rate dignity").[1] Its site is today occupied by a Turkish town, Akhisar, with a population of about fifty thousand.

### Inscriptions

A few inscriptions have been turned up. One of them is a letter from the proconsul or governor, P. Cornelius Scipio, dated 10–6 B.C., to the Thyateirans about a dispute involving either the tax-collectors, or more probably some temple lands which had been leased at a high rent.[2] An

---

1. R. C. Trench, *Commentary on the Epistles to the Seven Churches in Asia* (Minneapolis: Klock and Klock, 1978 reprint of the 1897 edition), p. 144.
2. R. K. Sherk, *Roman Documents from the Greek East* (Baltimore: Johns Hopkins University Press, 1969), pp. 338–40.

inscription from the early empire records that οἱ ἀλειφό-
μενοι (literally, "the anointed ones," i.e., the athletes) honored a Gaius Julius Marcus, the son of Lepidos, τὸν ἀρ-
χιερέα τῆς Ἀσίας καὶ ἀγωνοθέτην ("the high priest of Asia
and agōnothetēs").[3] There is a bilingual milestone dated to
A.D. 92 from the reign of Domitian.[4]

As the ancient site is occupied it has been subject to but
limited excavations. Otto Meinardus reports:

> Recent excavations at Tepe Mezari in the center of Ak-
> hisar, which have unearthed a section of a 2nd century
> A.D. Roman road and part of a stoa as well as the walls of a
> 6th century administrative building (?), may also reveal
> ruins of Christian buildings, throwing additional light
> upon the early Christian heritage of this city.[5]

### Guilds and Purple Cloth

As Thyateira is rarely mentioned in literature, our
knowledge of the city is based almost entirely upon inscriptions and coins. Inscriptions from the Julio-Claudian
era are almost nonexistent.[6] There are more inscriptions
from the Flavian era, especially milestones.[7] Coins from
Thyateira depict temples of Apollo Tyrimnaeus and Athe-
na/Roma, and the temple of Rome from the reign of
Severus Alexander.[8]

C. J. Hemer points out the one characteristic which does
emerge from the sources:

> Perhaps the one salient thing about Thyatira is the unusual
> prominence of trade-guilds in the few available sources.

3. *Documents Illustrating the Reigns of Augustus and Tiberius,* ed. V.
Ehrenberg and A. H. M. Jones, 2nd ed. (Oxford: Clarendon Press,
1976), p. 157, #353.

4. *Select Documents of the Principates of the Flavian Emperors,* ed. M.
McCrum and A. G. Woodhead, 2nd ed. (Cambridge: Cambridge University Press, 1966), p. 117, #422.

5. Otto F. A. Meinardus, *St. John of Patmos and the Seven Churches of the
Apocalypse* (Athens: Lycabettus, 1974), p. 100.

6. C. C. Vermeule, *Roman Imperial Art in Greece and Asia Minor* (Cambridge: Harvard University Press, 1968), p. 218.

7. Ibid., pp. 237, 462.

8. M. J. Price and B. L. Trell, *Coins and Their Cities* (Detroit: Wayne
State University Press, 1977), pp. 196, 269.

There are references to unions of clothiers, bakers, tanners, potters, linen-workers, wool-merchants, slave-traders, copper-smiths and dyers.[9]

Hemer analyzes the rare word *chalkolibanon* ("fine brass") in Revelation 1:15 and 2:18 as a reference to a special alloy of the local metalworkers.[10]

Among the most important guilds were those that worked with textiles. This was true not only at Thyateira, but also at Sardis, Miletus, Colossae, Laodicea, and Hierapolis.[11] We know also that working with textiles was one of the commonest occupations of the Jews in Asia Minor.[12]

When Paul preached at Philippi, he converted a woman from Thyateira named Lydia, who was a seller of purple cloth (Acts 16:14). The name *Lydia* no doubt originates from the fact that Thyateira was located in the territory of Lydia (see figures 1 and 2). Meinardus reports that in 1872 Professor Mertzides found in Philippi the following Greek text: "The city honored from among the purple dyers, an outstanding citizen, Antiochus, the son of Lykus, a native of Thyatira, as a benefactor."[13] David Magie observes that "Thyateira, in fact, seems to have been particularly important for its dyeing process, for its guild of dyers was evidently unusually prosperous."[14]

True purple dye, which was obtained from the murex shell fish by the Phoenicians and others, was the only color-fast dye known to the ancient world. Purple thus became the preeminent status symbol of royalty and of the wealthy. Shortly after Paul's ministry at Philippi the emperor Nero tried without success to interdict the highest

---

9. C. J. Hemer, "Unto the Angels of the Churches," *BH* 11 (1975): 110.

10. Ibid., pp. 113–14; cf. Robert H. Mounce, *The Book of Revelation* (Grand Rapids: Wm. B. Eerdmans, 1977), pp. 101–02.

11. David Magie, *Roman Rule in Asia Minor* (Princeton: Princeton University Press, 1950), vol. I, p. 47.

12. S. Safrai and M. Stern, eds., *The Jewish People in the First Century* (Philadelphia: Fortress Press, 1974), vol. I, p. 716. The word *Tarseus* was synonymous with linen weavers.

13. Meinardus, *St. John*, p. 93.

14. Magie, *Roman Rule*, vol. I, p. 48, n. 80.

qualities of purple except for imperial use.[15] In the 2nd century Dio Chrysostom still had cause to rebuke the politicians of Tarsus for their love of front-row seats, gold crowns, and purple robes.[16]

The purple cloth which was sold by Thyateirans such as Lydia, however, was not true purple.[17] The dyed cloth which she sold was no doubt colored with the local madder plant, which resulted in a pigment now known as "Turkey red."[18] When the art of obtaining true purple was lost with the fall of Constantinople in 1453, Pope Paul II decreed that the robes of cardinals would henceforth be dyed in the imitation purple derived from the insect cochineal (see p. 152).[19]

15.  Suetonius, De Vita Caesarum, "Nero" 32; M. Reinhold, "The History of Purple as a Status Symbol in Antiquity," Collection Latomus 116 (1970): 50; Wolfgang Born, "Purple in Classical Antiquity," CIBA Review 1–2 (1937–39): 110–19.

16.  C. P. Jones, The Roman World of Dio Chrysostom (Cambridge: Harvard University Press, 1978), p. 81.

17.  F. F. Bruce, Paul: Apostle of the Heart Set Free (Grand Rapids: Wm. B. Eerdmans, 1977), p. 220, errs on this point.

18.  W. M. Ramsay, Letters to the Seven Churches (Grand Rapids: Baker, 1979 reprint), pp. 325–26; Hemer, "Unto the Angels," p. 112.

19.  Reinhold, "Purple as a Status Symbol," p. 70.

# 4

## SMYRNA

### Location

Smyrna was located on the coast some 35 miles north of Ephesus on the border between Aeolis to the north and Ionia to the south. Smyrna was the terminus of a major route into the interior through the Hermus Valley past Sardis. In the Greco-Roman periods Smyrna had a population of over one hundred thousand.

Smyrna had in addition to the outer harbor a small inner basin which has long since silted up. The important Turkish port of Izmir conceals almost all traces of Smyrna's ancient remains.

### New Testament References

The only references to Smyrna are those in Revelation, where the site is one of the seven cities addressed by the Lord (Rev. 1:11; 2:8). In view of subsequent developments the warnings about sufferings and the hostility of the Jews are highly significant.

### Historical Background

Founded in the early first millennium B.C. by Aeolian

**IV.1**
Old Smyrna (7th–5th century B.C.) was located at Bayrakli, which is now in the midst of state-owned orchards.

immigrants from Greece, Smyrna eventually became an Ionian city during the archaic age. Tradition associated Homer with Smyrna. Excavations by J. M. Cook from 1948 to 1951 uncovered extensive remains of archaic Smyrna in the midst of state-owned orchards in an area known as Bayrakli (see photo IV.1).[1] The excavator found vivid evidence to confirm the attacks upon the city by the Lydians reported by Herodotus (I.14).

After a period of decline during the 6th and 5th centuries B.C., the city was refounded in the late 4th century on a new site about 3 miles south of the old city. Traditions report that Alexander offered to rebuild the town. It was Antigonus who established the Hellenistic settlement.

1. J. M. Cook, "Old Smyrna, 1948–51," *Annual of the British School at Athens* 53–54 (1958–59): 1–34; idem, *The Greeks in Ionia and the East* (New York: F. Praeger, 1963), pp. 70–74.

## The City's Beauty

By the 1st century B.C. Cicero could speak of Smyrna as one of the most flourishing towns of Asia, and Strabo could describe it as the finest of the Ionian cities. Known as ἄγαλμα τῆς ᾽Ασίας ("the ornament of Asia"), Smyrna was famed for its splendid paved streets. The orator Aelius Aristides boasted of the city:

> All the adornment intended for use, affording grateful rest to the body, and to the soul opportunity and ease for needful labours—has all arisen unitedly from temples, baths, harbours, race-courses. . . .[2]

The Neo-Pythagorean sage Apollonius of Tyana was also said to have commented on the external beauties of the city:

> He saw that the Smyrnaeans followed every kind of knowledge eagerly, and so he encouraged them and gave them more eagerness. They must put more pride in themselves, he told them, than in the appearance of their city; even if it was the most beautiful on earth, with the sea at its disposal and always supplied with a west wind, still its sons were a finer adornment than colonnades, pictures and excess of gold.[3]

## The Imperial Cult

In 195 B.C. Smyrna became the first city in Asia Minor to erect a temple for the cult of the city of Rome. In the early imperial period, when eleven cities from Asia competed for the honor of being selected *neōkoros* for the imperial cult, Tiberius selected Smyrna (Tacitus, *Annals* III.63; IV.56). Coins from Smyrna depict the temples to Rome, to Tiberius, and to Hadrian, as well as temples to Tyche and to Nemesis.[4] A coin from Domitian's reign depicts an octastyle temple.[5]

---

2. See C. J. Cadoux, *Ancient Smyrna* (Oxford: Basil Blackwell, 1938), p. 275.

3. Philostratus, *Life of Apollonius*, tr. C. P. Jones (Harmondsworth: Penguin, 1970), IV.7, p. 90.

4. M. J. Price and B. L. Trell, *Coins and Their Cities* (Detroit: Wayne State University Press, 1977), pp. 215, 268.

5. Ibid., p. 32.

Other materials illustrating Smyrna's loyalty to the emperors include a coin portraying Nero,[6] and dedications to Titus and Domitian. Statues of Domitian, Trajan, and Hadrian have also been recovered.[7] Some of these objects are displayed in the fine museum in Izmir.

## Public Monuments

An aqueduct was built at Smyrna by Trajan's father. Several copies of an inscription which describes the repairing of this aqueduct by the proconsul L. Baebius Tullus between 102 and 112 have been found.[8]

Polemo, the teacher of Aristides, who had been born in Laodicea but who settled at Smyrna, was able to persuade the emperor Hadrian to donate 250,000 drachmae to Smyrna. According to Philostratus the funds were used to build a grain market, the most magnificent gymnasium in Asia, and a great temple of Zeus overlooking the gulf.[9]

Though we know the approximate location of these structures, almost none of the beautiful public monuments of Greco-Roman Smyrna have been recovered except for the state agora. Today nothing remains of the theater, which once seated twenty thousand on the northwest slope of Mount Pagos,[10] or of the stadium on the west slope, though their outlines were still visible earlier in this century.[11] C. C. Vermeule explains:

Considering her commercial prosperity and her coins, Smyrna ought to have produced more traces of imperial art; but the Greco-Roman city has enjoyed nearly continu-

6. M. Grant, *Nero* (New York: American Heritage, 1970), p. 232.

7. C. C. Vermeule, *Roman Imperial Art in Greece and Asia Minor* (Cambridge: Harvard University Press, 1968), p. 468.

8. Ibid., p. 252.

9. David Magie, *Roman Rule in Asia Minor* (Princeton: Princeton University Press, 1950), vol. I, p. 615; Fergus Millar, *The Emperor in the Roman World* (London: Duckworth, 1977), pp. 421, 453.

10. Magie, *Roman Rule*, vol. II, p. 1446.

11. Cf. E. Akurgal, *Ancient Civilizations and Ruins of Turkey*, 2nd ed. (Istanbul: Mobil Oil Türk A.S., 1970), p. 121, with W. M. Ramsay, "Smyrna," *Encyclopedia Britannica* (11th ed., 1910), vol. XXV, p. 281.

**IV.2**
The agora of the Hellenistic-Roman city is located three miles south of Old Smyrna.

ous habitation through the Middle Ages to the present, and most ancient buildings disappeared long ago.[12]

The sole area of Greco-Roman Smyrna which has been excavated is the state agora, surrounded today by huddled houses. Between 1932 and 1941 Rudolf Naumann and Salahattin Kantar excavated the agora's large courtyard, 120 by 80 meters (394 by 262.5 feet), featuring a vaulted basement and a two-story portico (see photos IV.2 and 3).

In 177/178 a strong earthquake devastated much of the city. Aristides wrote an eloquent appeal to the emperor Marcus Aurelius, describing Smyrna—the glory of Asia—transformed into a waste. The emperor was so moved that he burst into tears. He granted the city a ten years' remission of taxes and funds for rebuilding.[13] Among the frag-

---

12. Vermeule, *Roman Imperial Art,* p. 70.
13. Magie, *Roman Rule,* vol. I, p. 666; Millar, *The Emperor,* pp. 208, 423; C. A. Behr, *Aelius Aristides and the Sacred Tales* (Amsterdam: A. M. Hakkert, 1968), pp. 112–13; Anthony Birley, *Marcus Aurelius* (Boston: Little, Brown, 1966), p. 281; G. W. Bowersock, *Greek Sophists in the Roman Empire* (Oxford: Clarendon Press, 1969), pp. 45–46.

**IV.3**
The columns of the agora date from a rebuilding in the 2nd
century A.D. after a powerful earthquake damaged the city.

ments recovered by the excavators were the keystone busts
of the imperial family, a marble triad of local divinities,
and inscriptions recording the imperial benefactions.[14]

## The Martyrdom of Polycarp

In the early 2nd century Smyrna was the home of a
vigorous Christian community. As Ignatius, bishop of
Antioch, traveled to Rome to be martyred in about 117, he
wrote letters to Smyrna and to its bishop, Polycarp.[15]

14. Vermeule, *Roman Imperial Art,* pp. 70, 270.
15.  M. A. Shepherd, "Smyrna in the Ignatius Letters," *Journal of Religion* 20 (1940): 141–59.

The aged Polycarp himself was to be martyred. The text which describes his death is the first of the martyr acts from the early church.[16] Eusebius dates his martyrdom to 166/167, a date favored by C. A. Behr.[17] Other scholars prefer the earlier date of 156, inasmuch as Irenaeus, the bishop of Lyons, who was born in Smyrna, attests that Polycarp knew St. John at Ephesus.[18]

When the proconsul Quadratus adjured Polycarp to deny Christ, the venerable bishop answered in memorable words:

> Eighty and six years have I served Him and He has done me no wrong. How then can I blaspheme my King who has saved me?[19]

Ten other Christians, including some from Philadelphia, were martyred along with Polycarp in the city's stadium.[20]

The letter to the church in Smyrna had warned: "I know the slander of those who say they are Jews and are not, but are a synagogue of Satan" (Rev. 2:9, NIV). One of the remarkable features of the martyrdom of Polycarp was the active role played by the Jews, who, though it was the Sabbath, helped to gather faggots for the fires.[21]

C. J. Hemer notes that "several inscriptions of the city attest the presence of a synagogue there."[22] A much discussed inscription from Hadrian's reign (123/124) makes

---

16. W. R. Schoedel, *Polycarp, Martyrdom of Polycarp, Fragments of Papias* (Camden: Thomas Nelson & Sons, 1967), p. 47.

17. See Behr, *Aelius Aristides*, pp. 98–101, for a defense of this later date.

18. H. Chadwick, *The Early Church* (Baltimore: Penguin, 1967), p. 30; R. M. Grant, *The Apostolic Fathers* (New York: Thomas Nelson & Sons, 1964), p. 71.

19. Kirsopp Lake in the Loeb edition of *The Apostolic Fathers* (London: W. Heinemann, 1913), vol. II, p. 325, n. 2, comments: "βασιλεύς represents 'imperator' not 'rex,' and though it can hardly be translated 'Emperor,' the antithesis to Caesar is clearly implied."

20. See Cadoux, *Ancient Smyrna*, p. 358, for a photo of the stadium area.

21. W. M. Ramsay, *Letters to the Seven Churches* (Grand Rapids: Baker, 1979 reprint), p. 273.

22. C. J. Hemer, "Unto the Angels of the Churches," *BH* 11 (1975): 62.

an enigmatic reference to a contribution of ten thousand drachmae for some public purpose by οἱ ποτὲ Ἰουδαῖοι ("those who were once Jews"). There are three possible interpretations: (1) the view that these were renegade Jews (so Böckh, Lightfoot, Schürer); (2) the view that these were Gentile proselytes who had reverted to their former beliefs (so Schultze, Cadoux);[23] and (3) the view that this refers to the fact that the Jewish community was no longer recognized as a legally constituted entity after A.D. 70 (so Mommsen, La Piana, Ramsay, Hemer).[24]

A century after Polycarp's martyrdom the empire-wide persecutions of Decius (250) resulted in the apostasy of the bishop of Smyrna, Euktemon. But the elder Pionios went bravely to his death, addressing his final words to those "men who boast about Smyrna's beauty, who revere Homer . . . and those Jews who are present."[25] A graphic description of his crucifixion has been preserved for us in the *Acta Pionii*.

23. Cadoux, *Ancient Smyrna,* p. 348.
24. Ramsay, *Letters to the Seven Churches,* p. 272; Hemer, "Unto the Angels," p. 62.
25. Cadoux, *Ancient Smyrna,* p. 382.

# 5

## SARDIS

### Location

Sardis, the capital of Lydia, is located 45 miles to the east of Smyrna in the Hermus River valley (see figures 1 and 2). The modern highway between Izmir and Afyon passes through the village of Sart, which still retains the ancient name.

### New Testament References

Sardis appears only in Revelation as one of the seven churches to which letters are addressed (Rev. 1:11; 3:1, 4). C. J. Hemer believes that the references in Revelation may allude to the illustrious history of the city.[1]

### Historical Background

After the destruction of the Phrygian capital of Gordium by the invading Cimmerians in about 700 B.C., the dominant power in Asia Minor became the Lydian Kingdom with its capital at Sardis. The first king of the

---

1. C. J. Hemer, "The Sardis Letter and the Croesus Tradition," *New Testament Studies* 19 (1972–73): 94–97.

# RUINS OF SARDIS

## Figure 4

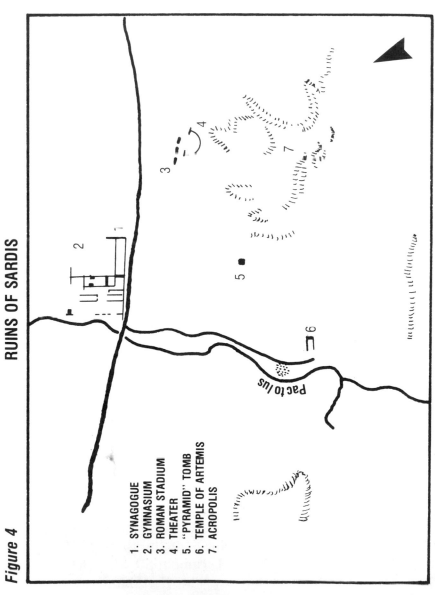

1. SYNAGOGUE
2. GYMNASIUM
3. ROMAN STADIUM
4. THEATER
5. "PYRAMID" TOMB
6. TEMPLE OF ARTEMIS
7. ACROPOLIS

Pactolus

After Ekrem Akurgal, *Ancient Civilizations and Ruins of Turkey*, 2nd ed. (Istanbul: Mobil Oil Türk A.S., 1970)

Mermnad Dynasty, Gyges (687–652 B.C.),[2] is credited with the invention of coinage.[3] The recent excavations have uncovered but a sliver of an early Lydian coin.[4]

Just to the north of Sardis and south of the Gygean Lake is the royal Lydian cemetery known as Bin Tepe ("Thousand Hills"), where there are about a hundred tumuli. G. M. A. Hanfmann explored the interior of the Tumulus of Gyges from 1963 to 1966, but was not able to find the burial chamber.[5]

Croesus (560–546 B.C.), the most famous Lydian king, was noted for his fabulous gold, panned from the sands of the Pactolus stream.[6] In 1968 the excavators found nearly three hundred crucibles for refining gold, thus lending substance to the ancient tradition.[7] Among the very few gold objects which have been recovered are a tiny gold ram[8] and gold thread from a textile of the Roman period.[9]

Cyrus captured Sardis in 546 B.C. and according to Herodotus spared the life of Croesus. Though some scholars believe that there may be a basis for this tradi-

2. These are the traditional dates according to the Armenian version of Eusebius. A. J. Spalinger, "The Date of Gyges and Its Historical Implications," *Journal of the American Oriental Society* 98 (1978): 400–449, argues for a later date for Gyges's death (644 B.C.).

3. See E. M. Yamauchi, *Greece and Babylon* (Grand Rapids: Baker, 1967), pp. 59–60.

4. G. M. A. Hanfmann, *Letters from Sardis* (Cambridge: Harvard University Press, 1972), pp. 125–26; C. H. Greenewalt, "The Eighteenth Campaign at Sardis (1975)," *Bulletin of the American Schools of Oriental Research* 228 (1977): 54–56.

5. G. M. A. Hanfmann, "The Tomb of Gyges," *Illustrated London News,* 20 March 1965, pp. 26–27; idem and J. Waldbaum, *A Survey of Sardis and the Major Monuments Outside the City Walls* (Cambridge: Harvard University Press, 1976), p. 4.

6. John G. Pedley, *Sardis in the Age of Croesus* (Norman: University of Oklahoma Press, 1969). For a photo of the Pactolus, see Hanfmann, *Letters,* p. 50.

7. Hanfmann, *Letters,* pp. 228–29; W. J. Young, "The Fabulous Gold of the Pactolus Valley," *Bulletin of the Museum of Fine Arts, Boston* 70 (1972): 4–13.

8. Hanfmann, *Letters,* p. 227.

9. G. M. A. Hanfmann, "Sardis, 1975," *AS* 26 (1976): 61.

tion,[10] the Chaldean Chronicles seem to indicate that Cyrus killed the Lydian king.[11]

Sardis was to remain the capital of the Persian satrapy of western Asia Minor until the campaign of Alexander liberated the Ionian Greeks. One striking monument from the Persian era is a pyramid tomb discovered on the slopes of a hill north of the temple of Artemis which bears a striking resemblance to the famous tomb of Cyrus at Pasargadae.[12]

After the battle of Ipsus Sardis fell under Seleucid domination from 270 to 190 B.C. When the Romans defeated Antiochus III, they gave Sardis to the Pergamene king, Eumenes II, in 188 B.C. In 133 B.C. Sardis came into the Roman orbit along with other Pergamene territories.

Sardis joined other Asian cities in honoring the Roman emperors. Augustus is named in twenty-one inscriptions.[13] When his grandson Gaius assumed the toga of manhood in 5 B.C., the city sent a delegation to convey its felicitations. We possess the text of the decree enacted by the council and people of Sardis. They determined:

> to send ambassadors from among the most distinguished men to offer greetings from the city, to hand over to him [Gaius] a copy of this decree, sealed with the public seal, and to address Augustus on matters of common interest to Asia and to the city.[14]

We also possess the emperor's letter to Sardis, acknowledging his gratitude for the decree. R. K. Sherk comments, "Behind it one can see a ruler busy with the de-

10. Max Mallowan, "Cyrus the Great," *Iran* 10 (1972): 1–17.

11. D. J. Wiseman, *The Chaldaean Chronicles* (London: British Museum, 1956).

12. Hanfmann, *Letters,* pp. 259–60.

13. C. C. Vermeule, *Roman Imperial Art in Greece and Asia Minor* (Cambridge: Harvard University Press, 1968), p. 461.

14. Fergus Millar, *The Emperor in the Roman World* (London: Duckworth, 1977), p. 217; Donald Earl, *The Age of Augustus* (New York: Crown, 1968), pp. 178–80.

mands of empire but still interested and courteous enough
to dictate or write an answer to an expression of loyalty."[15]

In the year A.D. 17 during the reign of Tiberius a dev-
astating earthquake destroyed twelve Asian cities. Tacitus
(*Annals* II.47) reports:

> The same year twelve important cities of Asia collapsed in
> an earthquake during the night, so that the devastation was
> all the more unexpected and crushing. . . . The disaster was
> harshest to the citizens of Sardis, and brought them the
> largest share of pity; for Tiberius promised them ten mil-
> lion sesterces and remitted for five years whatever they
> used to pay to the public exchequer or his privy purse.[16]

Other sources report that immense mountains settled, that
plains were heaved on high, and that fires broke out in the
ruins. The granting of aid to these cities was commemorated by a coin issued in Rome in 22 with the inscription
*Civitatibus Asiae Restitutis.* In 30 a statue was set up to
Tiberius in Puteoli with a list of the Asian cities inscribed
on the base.[17]

A bilingual inscription lists the names of individuals and
corporations who received water from an aqueduct completed by a gift from Claudius.[18] Though there are many
other inscriptions from the reigns of various emperors, the
statues or fragments of statues which have been recovered
are of the later emperors—Antoninus Pius, Lucius Verus,
Caracalla, and Severus Alexander.[19]

15. R. K. Sherk, *Roman Documents from the Greek East* (Baltimore: Johns
Hopkins University Press, 1969), p. 68.
16. This and other classical passages are conveniently collected in *Ancient Literary Sources on Sardis,* ed. John G. Pedley (Cambridge: Harvard
University Press, 1972), p. 64; G. M. A. Hanfmann, *From Croesus to
Constantine* (Ann Arbor: University of Michigan Press, 1975), pp.
42–43; and David Magie, *Roman Rule in Asia Minor* (Princeton: Princeton University Press, 1950), vol. I, p. 500. Next to Sardis the greatest
damage was inflicted upon Magnesia. The names of the other ten cities
are not the same in the classical sources. See N. N. Ambraseys, "Value of
Historical Records of Earthquakes," *Nature* 232 (Aug. 6, 1977): 377–78.
17. Magie, *Roman Rule,* vol. II, p. 1358.
18. Vermeule, *Roman Imperial Art,* p. 461; V. M. Scramuzza, *The Emperor Claudius* (Cambridge: Harvard University Press, 1940), p. 160.
19. Vermeule, *Roman Imperial Art,* p. 461.

## Excavations

From 1910 to 1914 Howard Crosby Butler cleared the area of the Artemis temple (figure 4, #6) for Princeton University. Butler also opened up more than 1,100 Lydian graves but found objects in only seventy of them. Excavations were resumed in 1958 by the American Schools of Oriental Research, Harvard University, and Cornell University under the direction of G. M. A. Hanfmann and have continued to the present.[20]

Nearly three hundred pieces of sculpture have been recovered from Sardis, both from the excavations and from chance finds.[21] Even with over twenty years of excavations, many structures still need to be cleared, including the theater (which could hold twenty thousand spectators), the stadium, and major public buildings east of the gymnasium. Hanfmann suggests that the unexcavated palace of Croesus may possibly lie under a hill now topped by a Byzantine fort just 200 meters (656 feet) west of the theater.[22]

## Deities and Temples

The patron deities of Sardis were Cybele and Artemis. W. M. Ramsay had held that the Greek Artemis and the Anatolian Cybele were but forms of the same goddess.[23] New iconographic evidence shows that the goddesses were distinct. On a reused block recovered from the synagogue

---

20. Annual reports have appeared in the *Bulletin of the American Schools of Oriental Research*. The literature is quite extensive; see Hanfmann, *Letters,* pp. 345–49; for major recent articles see "Sardis" in the *IDBS*. For an interim summary, see D. G. Mitten, "A New Look at Ancient Sardis," *BA* 29 (1966): 37–68. I have profited from a paper by David Walker prepared for my graduate seminar.

21. G. M. A. Hanfmann and N. H. Ramage, *Sculpture from Sardis* (Cambridge: Harvard University Press, 1978).

22. Hanfmann, *Letters,* p. 326.

23. W. M. Ramsay, *Letters to the Seven Churches* (Grand Rapids: Baker, 1979 reprint), pp. 363–64; idem, *The Social Basis of Roman Power in Asia Minor* (Amsterdam: A. M. Hakkert, 1967), p. 113.

Artemis is shown holding a deer while Cybele holds a lion.[24]

The great temple in Sardis was the one dedicated to Artemis. The archaic temple built by Croesus was destroyed in 499 B.C. during the Ionian Revolt (Herodotus V.102). It is the fourth largest Ionic-style temple, though it was never completely finished. It measures about 300 by 160 feet. Two of the seventy-eight columns, 58 feet high, still stand. The earthquake of A.D. 17 covered the temple with landslides.[25]

Coins from the reigns of Marcus Aurelius, Commodus, and Elagabalus depict the temple and the cult image of Artemis.[26] Still other coins depict sanctuaries which have not yet been identified: (1) the sanctuary of Aphrodite Paphia on a coin of Hadrian;[27] (2) two neocorate temples on a coin of Septimius Severus;[28] (3) the great altar of Zeus Lydios on a coin of Elagabalus;[29] (4) a great altar with statues of Heracles and Zeus Lydios on a coin of Philip.[30]

## The Jews and the Synagogue

Though the three references to Sardis in the New Testament do not refer to the Jews of the city, there is abundant extrabiblical evidence for their presence. The Jewish community may have originated from the transfer of Jewish veterans from Mesopotamia to Lydia by Antiochus III.

---

24. G. M. A. Hanfmann and J. C. Waldbaum, "Kybele and Artemis," *Arch* 22 (1969): 264–69; Hanfmann, *Letters*, p. 239. Cf. A. Henrichs, "Despoina Kybele: Ein Beitrag zur religiösen Namenkunde," *Harvard Studies in Classical Philology* 80 (1976): 253–86; M. Vermaseren, *Cybele and Attis* (London: Thames & Hudson, 1977).

25. Hanfmann, *Letters*, p. 7; E. Akurgal, *Ancient Civilizations and Ruins of Turkey*, 2nd ed. (Istanbul: Mobil Oil Türk A.S., 1970), p. 124.

26. M. J. Price and B. L. Trell, *Coins and Their Cities* (Detroit: Wayne State University Press, 1977), p. 136.

27. Ibid., p. 28.

28. Ibid., p. 49.

29. Ibid., pp. 49, 138.

30. Ibid., p. 138.

Josephus cites two important documents from the time of Julius Caesar, confirming Jewish privileges in the city. In one of them the proconsul Gaius Norbanus Flaccus sent word to the council of Sardis: "Caesar has written to me, ordering that the Jews shall not be prevented from collecting sums of money, however great they may be, in accordance with their ancestral custom, and sending them up to Jerusalem" (*Antiquities* XVI.171).

**V.1** The reconstructed Marble Hall complex.

The other document is a decree passed by the council of Sardis to confirm the privileges of the Jews. This document presents us with the most detailed information we have on a Jewish community in Asia.

> Whereas the Jewish citizens living in our city have continually received many great privileges from the people and have now come before the council and the people and have pleaded that as their laws and freedom have been restored to them by the Roman Senate and people, they may, in accordance with their accepted customs, come together and have a communal life and adjudicate suits among themselves, and that a place be given them in which they may gather together with their wives and children and offer their ancestral prayers and sacrifices to God, it has therefore been decreed by the council and people that

permission shall be given them to come together on stated days to do those things which are in accordance with their laws, and also that a place shall be set apart by the magistrates for them to build and inhabit... and that the market-officials of the city shall be charged with the duty of having suitable food for them brought in.[31] (*Antiq.* XIV.259ff.)

Several inscriptions have been recovered from Sardis which attest to the role of the Jews as goldsmiths, shopkeepers, and so on. Nine Jews are even listed as *bouleutēs,* that is, as members of the city's council.[32]

In 1962 as the excavators were clearing the huge urban complex called the Marble Hall, which included baths and a gymnasium (see photos V.1 and 2), just north of the highway, they uncovered a huge building which has turned out to be the largest synagogue ever discovered (see figure 4, #1, and photo V.3). After clearing operations in 1963, the excavators spent many seasons carefully restoring the building and its beautiful paneled decorations.[33]

A careful examination of the levels indicates that the building went through four stages (see figure 5).[34]

*Stage 1:* The building originally had three rooms which were used either as dressing rooms or as lecture halls of the gymnasium-palaestra complex, built at some time after the earthquake of 17.

*Stage 2:* In the 2nd century the building was transformed into a civic basilica. Fragments of a Hebrew inscription honoring the imperial colleague of Marcus Aurelius, Verus (c. 166), may point to either a gift or a sale

31. See A. Kraabel, "Judaism in Asia Minor" (Th.D. dissertation, Harvard University, 1968). I have not been able to obtain L. Roth-Gerson, "The Civil and the Religious Status of the Jews in Asia Minor" (Ph.D. dissertation, Hebrew University, 1972).

32. Hanfmann, *Letters,* p. 100; S. Safrai and M. Stern, eds., *The Jewish People in the First Century* (Philadelphia: Fortress Press, 1974), p. 479. Louis Robert, *Nouvelles inscriptions de Sardes I* (Paris: A. Maisonneuve, 1964), pp. 54–55.

33. Hanfmann, *Letters,* p. 216.

34. A. R. Seager, "The Building History of the Sardis Synagogue," *AJA* 76 (1972): 425–35.

**V.2** Details of the restored Marble Hall.

**Figure 5**     **SYNAGOGUE AT SARDIS**

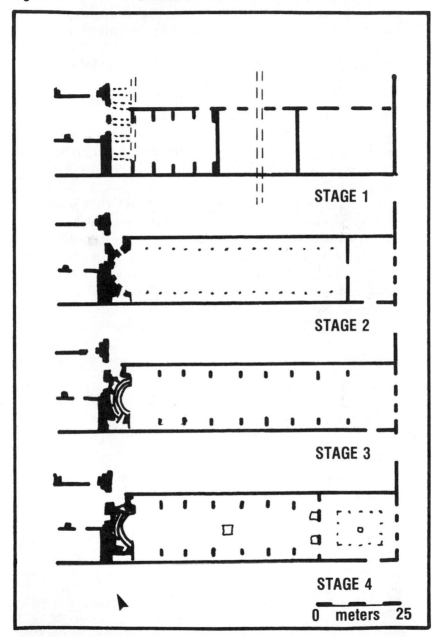

After G. M. A. Hanfmann, *From Croesus to Constantine* (Ann Arbor: University of Michigan Press, 1975), figure 116. Reprinted by permission of the publishers.

of the building to the Jews. A. H. Detweiler speculates that the building was turned over to the Jews in gratitude for their assistance in rebuilding the city after the earthquake.[35]

*Stage 3:* The third stage (170–250?) involved the first use of the building as a synagogue.

*Stage 4:* Renovations were made (350–400) with the eastern end of the building partitioned off as a colonnaded forecourt (see photo V.4).[36] In this stage the main hall extended 60 by 18 meters (197 by 59 feet), with an additional 40 meters (131 feet) occupied by the forecourt and the porch.[37]

More than eighty Jewish inscriptions in Greek have been recovered; three Hebrew texts include one which contains the word *shalom*.[38] The prominence and strength of the Jewish community at Sardis, which these inscriptions now attest, may explain the vehement anti-Jewish tone of the famous Easter sermon, *Peri Pascha*, delivered by Melito, bishop of Sardis (2nd century).[39] The text of this sermon was recovered only in 1937 among the Bodmer Papyri.[40]

Melito was involved in the Quartodeciman controversy over the date of Easter. The Asian churches followed the

---

35. The Jews certainly had a synagogue at Sardis as early as the 1st century B.C., as indicated by Josephus, and as confirmed by an inscription listing the fountains of the city. See Safrai, *Jewish People*, p. 479.

36. Hanfmann, *Letters*, p. 323, plate V.

37. On the mosaics of the forecourt, see Andrew Ramage, "The Fourteenth Campaign at Sardis (1971)," *Bulletin of the American Schools of Oriental Research* 206 (1972): 37–39.

38. Hanfmann, *Letters*, p. 119.

39. A. G. Kraabel, "Melito the Bishop and the Synagogue at Sardis: Text and Context," in *Studies Presented to George M. A. Hanfmann*, ed. D. G. Mitten, J. G. Pedley, and J. A. Scott (Mainz: P. von Zabern, 1972), pp. 77–85. An inscription from the 1st century has been interpreted as a Christian text as it proclaims, "He is living." See E. M. Blaiklock, *The Cities of the New Testament* (London: Pickering & Inglis, 1965), p. 118.

40. F. V. Filson, "More Bodmer Papyri," *BA* 25 (1962): 50–57. For a new translation of Melito's sermon, see G. F. Hawthorne, "A New English Translation of Melito's Paschal Homily," in *Current Issues in*

**V.3** The huge Jewish synagogue.

**V.4** The forecourt of the synagogue.

Jewish custom of dating the Passover on the 14th of Nisan and celebrating Easter three days thereafter (no matter where in the week it might come), whereas the Western churches celebrated Easter on the Sunday after Passover. Melito is also noted as one of the earliest pilgrims to the Holy Land.

*Biblical and Patristic Interpretation,* ed. G. F. Hawthorne (Grand Rapids: Wm. B. Eerdmans, 1975), pp. 147–75; idem, "The Man Was Christ," *Christianity Today* 22 (March 24, 1978): 23–26.

# 6

## PHILADELPHIA

The city of Philadelphia was located east of Sardis (figure 2) on the route into the interior from Smyrna. It was also connected by a direct route to Thyateira north of Sardis, a route which was wrongly doubted by Ramsay.[1] The ancient sites of the theater and the stadium are now covered by the town of Alashehir.[2]

In the New Testament the city is mentioned only as one of the seven churches of Revelation (1:11; 3:7).

Philadelphia, which was built by Attalus Philadelphus or named after him by his brother Eumenes in the 2nd century B.C., does not figure very prominently in historical texts. According to R. C. Trench, "No city of Asia Minor

---

1. G. M. A. Hanfmann and J. Waldbaum, *A Survey of Sardis and the Major Monuments Outside the City Walls* (Cambridge: Harvard University Press, 1976), p. 170, n. 10.
2. Robert H. Mounce, *The Book of Revelation* (Grand Rapids: Wm. B. Eerdmans, 1977), p. 120; Otto F. A. Meinardus, *St. John of Patmos and the Seven Churches of the Apocalypse* (Athens: Lycabettus, 1974), p. 121.

suffered more, or so much, from violent and often-recurring earthquakes."[3] C. J. Hemer visited the site after the earthquake of 1969 had destroyed numerous houses and buildings.[4]

Apart from a statue of Pompey and one of Hadrian, and a stele of Caracalla,[5] our archaeological evidence is limited to numismatic representations of numerous temples including those of Artemis Anaitis (the Persian Anahita), Artemis Ephesia, Helios, Dionysus, Zeus, and Aphrodite.[6]

Ignatius passed through Philadelphia on his way to Smyrna and addressed one of his letters to the church there. Philadelphian Christians were martyred along with Polycarp. Philadelphia may have been one of the sources for the charismatic movement of Montanism, as one of the earliest places where Montanus prophesied was at Ardabav, which was probably but 15 miles up the Hermus Valley from Philadelphia.[7] The movement, which was more sectarian than heretical,[8] gained the adherence of the great North African apologist Tertullian in his later years.[9]

3. R. C. Trench, *Commentary on the Epistles to the Seven Churches in Asia* (Minneapolis: Klock and Klock, 1978 reprint of the 1897 edition), p. 181.

4. C. J. Hemer, "Unto the Angels of the Churches," *BH* 11 (1975): 172.

5. C. C. Vermeule, *Roman Imperial Art in Greece and Asia Minor* (Cambridge: Harvard University Press, 1968), p. 461.

6. M. J. Price and B. L. Trell, *Coins and Their Cities* (Detroit: Wayne State University Press, 1977), p. 267.

7. W. M. Calder, "Philadelphia and Montanism," *Bulletin of the John Rylands Library* 7 (1923): 309–54.

8. D. F. Wright, "Why Were the Montanists Condemned?" *Themelios* 2 (1976): 15–21.

9. T. D. Barnes, *Tertullian* (Oxford: Oxford University Press, 1971).

# 7

## EPHESUS

### Location

Ephesus was located at the mouth of the Cayster River on the coast between Smyrna and Miletus at the crossroads of the Ionian, Lydian, and Carian worlds (see figure 2). In the New Testament Era it was probably the fourth greatest city in the world (after Rome, Alexandria, and Antioch) with a population of about 250,000.

According to Pliny the Elder the sea used to wash up to the very edge of the city. The Roman harbor came up to the end of the Arcadian Road (see figure 6, #8). Because of the silt brought down by the river, the shore is now 6 miles away. Today the land between the ruins and the coast is planted in cotton.

Because of the lack of tides in the Mediterranean to scour out the detritus, the problem of sediment always plagued Ephesus and other harbors at the mouths of rivers. As early as 499 B.C. the Greek forces joining the Ionian Revolt found that they could not disembark their forces at the mouth of the Cayster. Eusebius (*Historia Ecclesiastica* IX.4.2) wrote that in A.D. 129 the council of Ephesus honored Hadrian for helping to make the harbor

## Figure 6        PLAN OF EPHESUS

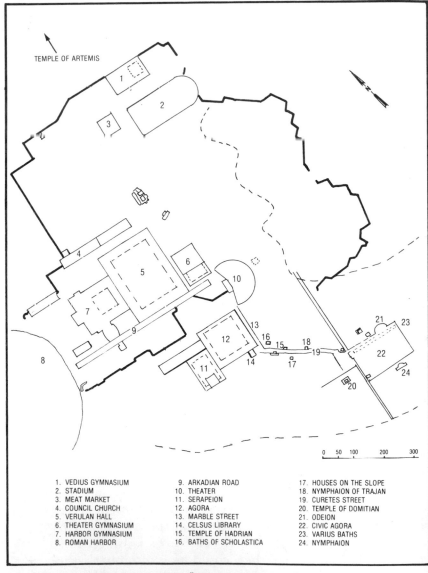

TEMPLE OF ARTEMIS

| | | |
|---|---|---|
| 1. VEDIUS GYMNASIUM | 9. ARKADIAN ROAD | 17. HOUSES ON THE SLOPE |
| 2. STADIUM | 10. THEATER | 18. NYMPHAION OF TRAJAN |
| 3. MEAT MARKET | 11. SERAPEION | 19. CURETES STREET |
| 4. COUNCIL CHURCH | 12. AGORA | 20. TEMPLE OF DOMITIAN |
| 5. VERULAN HALL | 13. MARBLE STREET | 21. ODEION |
| 6. THEATER GYMNASIUM | 14. CELSUS LIBRARY | 22. CIVIC AGORA |
| 7. HARBOR GYMNASIUM | 15. TEMPLE OF HADRIAN | 23. VARIUS BATHS |
| 8. ROMAN HARBOR | 16. BATHS OF SCHOLASTICA | 24. NYMPHAION |

After Anton Bammer, *Die Architektur des jüngeren Artemision von Ephesus* (Wiesbaden: F. Steiner, 1972)

navigable by diverting the Cayster. The proconsul of Asia under Marcus Aurelius reported that the emperor was constantly sending letters about the maintenance of the harbor.[1]

## New Testament References

Apart from the references to Ephesus in Revelation 1:11 and 2:1 and Paul's letter to the Ephesians, the most important passage is Acts 19, which describes Paul's three-year ministry (Acts 20:31) in Ephesus.[2]

The accuracy of Luke's description has been pointed out by W. M. Ramsay in numerous works, and has been reaffirmed by the distinguished classical scholar, A. N. Sherwin-White.[3]

Parallels to the mob scene at Ephesus may be found in the speeches of the orator, Dio Chrysostom, who lived in western Asia Minor in the second half of the 1st century (b. 40—d. after 112). In his "Euboean Discourse" (VII.25–26), Dio described a mob which had gathered in a theater to hear the case of a hunter:

> This wrath of theirs was something terrible, and they at once frightened the men against whom they raised their voices, so that some of them ran about begging for mercy, while others threw off their cloaks through fear. I too myself was once almost knocked over by the shouting, as though a tidal wave or thunder-storm had suddenly broken over me.[4] (Cf. Acts 19:32ff.)

The concern of the magistrate that the riot against Paul might harm the relations between Ephesus and Rome (Acts 19:40ff.) is paralleled by Dio's words to an angry mob

1. Fergus Millar, *The Emperor in the Roman World* (London: Duckworth, 1977), p. 9, n. 60.
2. For earlier studies, see W. M. Ramsay, "St. Paul at Ephesus," *The Expositor*, 4th series, 2 (1890): 1–22; G. S. Duncan, *St. Paul's Ephesian Ministry* (London: Hodder & Stoughton, 1929); F. V. Filson, "Ephesus and the New Testament," *BA* 8 (1945): 73–80.
3. A. N. Sherwin-White, *Roman Society and Roman Law in the New Testament* (Oxford: Clarendon Press, 1963), pp. 86–89.
4. C. P. Jones, *The Roman World of Dio Chrysostom* (Cambridge: Harvard University Press, 1978), pp. 21, 58.

who rioted over grain prices in his hometown of Prusa (XLVI.14):

> Nothing that happens in the cities goes unnoticed by the leaders, I mean the leaders superior to those here; just as the families of little children who are naughty at home report them to their teachers, so the misbehaviour of the assemblies is reported to them.[5]

In the 2nd century there was a further disturbance at Ephesus over a strike by the bakers. David Magie recounts:

> A more serious situation occurred at Ephesus, where a strike of the "brotherhood" of the bakers was attended with so much "disorder and tumult" that action was taken by an official, probably the proconsul, who, in order to prevent further violence, issued an edict forbidding the organization to hold unauthorized meetings or cause further disturbance and also commanding the bakers "to obey the regulations made for the general welfare."[6]

## Historical Background

Ancient Ephesus passed through three major periods: (1) the archaic period (900–560 B.C.) from its foundations until its subjection under the Lydian king Croesus; (2) the Greco-Lydian period (560–290 B.C.) until its occupation by Lysimachus, one of the successors of Alexander; (3) the Greco-Roman era (from 290 B.C. on).[7]

In the archaic period, though not as renowned as Miletus, Ephesus played a role in the Ionian Renaissance with such luminaries as Heraclitus the philosopher and Hipponax the poet.[8] After Croesus conquered the city

---

5. Cited by Jones, *Roman World,* p. 24. For other parallels, see G. Mussies, ed., *Dio Chrysostom and the New Testament* (Leiden: E. J. Brill, 1972).

6. David Magie, *Roman Rule in Asia Minor* (Princeton: Princeton University Press, 1950), vol. I, p. 635.

7. J. Keil, *Ephesos: Ein Führer durch die Ruinenstätte und ihre Geschichte,* 5th ed. (Vienna: Österreichisches Archäologisches Institut, 1964), p. 13.

8. John A. Cramer, *A Geographical and Historical Description of Asia Minor* (Amsterdam: A. M. Hakkert, 1971 reprint of the 1832 edition), p. 373.

(Herodotus I.26), he erected the archaic temple to Artemis. According to ancient tradition, which may be accurate, the temple was set on fire by Herostratos to gain a name for himself on the very day that Alexander the Great was born, that is, July 20, 356 B.C.[9] Some years later, in 334, when Alexander offered to rebuild the temple, the Ephesians declined his offer and rebuilt it themselves, with the women sacrificing their jewelry to provide funds.

After Lysimachus was killed in 281 B.C., Ephesus came under the control of the Seleucids. When the latter were defeated by the Romans at the battle of Magnesia (189 B.C.), Ephesus was given to Pergamum. In 133 Ephesus fell under the direct aegis of the Romans.

A statue of Julius Caesar has been found at Ephesus.[10] Mark Antony and Cleopatra spent the winter of 33–32 B.C. at Ephesus. In 1970 a colossal head of Antony was found in the upper civic agora.[11] It is probable that Antony and Cleopatra established the Egyptian temple which has been cleared in the northeast corner of the civic agora. Austrian excavators found there the stone head of the Egyptian god Ammon and the bell of a sistrum.[12]

A sanctuary dedicated to Rome and Augustus was enclosed within the precincts of the Artemision (temple of Artemis). It is depicted on Ephesian cistophori coins.[13] The triple gate which led from the commercial agora to the Library of Celsus was dedicated by two freedmen of

---

9. Plutarch, *Alexander* III.5. See J. R. Hamilton, *Plutarch: Alexander, A Commentary* (Oxford: Clarendon Press, 1969), p. 7.

10. C. C. Vermeule, *Roman Imperial Art in Greece and Asia Minor* (Cambridge: Harvard University Press, 1968), p. 463.

11. M. J. Mellink, "Archaeology in Asia Minor," *AJA* 75 (1971): 175.

12. E. Fossel, "Zur Tempel auf dem Staatsmarkt in Ephesos," *Hauptblatt* 50 (1972–73): 212–19.

To the southwest of the commercial agora a Serapeum (figure 6, #11), 29.2 by 37 meters (95 by 121 feet), was set in a large courtyard. It contained inscriptions which mention Serapis, Isis, and Anubis. See Keil, *Ephesos*, p. 102; R. Salditt-Trappmann, *Tempel der ägyptischen Götter in Griechenland und an der Westküste Kleinasiens* (Leiden: E. J. Brill, 1970), ch. 2.

13. Magie, *Roman Rule*, vol. I, p. 470; Vermeule, *Roman Imperial Art*, p. 218.

**VII.1**
The temple of Domitian was located on the right at the top of Curetes Street.

Agrippa, Mazaeus and Mithridates, in 4 or 3 B.C. to Augustus, Agrippa, Livia, and Julia, as may be seen in the inscription at the site.[14] In 1972 a portrait head, which represents one of Augustus's grandsons—either Gaius or Lucius—was discovered in the Varius Baths.[15]

Nero, who was a great admirer of Greek culture and was enthusiastic about the stage and about athletics, rebuilt the stadium at Ephesus. For his benefactions, Ephesus commemorated Nero on a coin.[16] At the same time Nero ransacked Ephesus (as he did other cities) for statues for his own collection.

It was above all Domitian—the oppressive emperor under whom John was exiled to Patmos—who made his presence known at Ephesus. At the upper end of Curetes Street (see figure 6, #20, and photo VII.1) on a large terrace, 50 by 100 meters (164 by 328 feet), a great altar

---

14. Vermeule, *Roman Imperial Art,* p. 219.
15. M. J. Mellink, "Archaeology in Asia Minor," *AJA* 78 (1974): 123.
16. Michael Grant, *Nero* (New York: American Heritage, 1970), p. 238.

**VII.2**
The colossal statue of the emperor Domitian (A.D. 81–96) is now on display in the Izmir (Smyrna) Museum.

and temple were erected to Domitian.[17] Magie, arguing from the dates of the proconsuls listed in the dedications, suggests that this temple may have been set up as an imperial temple under Domitian's father, Vespasian.[18]

When Domitian was assassinated in 96, the Ephesians probably destroyed the emperor's colossal marble statue, the head and forearm of which have been recovered. The statue was four times life-size with the forearm extending to a man's height (see photo VII.2). C. C. Vermeule comments, "The colossal marble head and arm of the Izmir

17. Keil, *Ephesos,* pp. 124–26; H. Vetters, "Domitianterrasse und Domitiangasse," *Beiblatt* 50 (1972–75): 311–30.
18. Magie, *Roman Rule,* vol. II, pp. 1432–34.

Museum from the Flavian temple of Ephesus is one of the grandest ensembles in the East."[19]

Trajan took great interest in Ephesus as his father Marcus Ulpius Trajanus had been appointed proconsul of Asia in 79. His father rebuilt the wall surrounding the Artemision precinct. Trajan's most conspicuous contribution was a two-story nymphaion or fountain house on Curetes Street, which was once adorned with colossal statues (see figure 6, #18).

The well-traveled emperor Hadrian regarded Ephesus as his favorite city. Games named the Hadrianea were sponsored in his honor. It was in his reign that Ephesus was made the imperial capital of Asia (A.D. 125), superseding Pergamum.

The city's second neocorate temple was dedicated to Hadrian in 129.[20] This has usually been identified with the temple with the rounded arch discovered on Curetes Street in 1956 (see figure 6, #15). E. L. Bowie, however, argues that this structure was only a shrine dedicated by a private individual to the emperor, inasmuch as the numismatic evidence which depicts the four neocorate temples[21] does not depict a structure with a rounded arch.[22]

Ephesus honored the emperor Antoninus Pius by celebrating his birthday with spectacles and the distribution of silver. This is revealed by an important inscription found in the theater, first published by Theodor Mommsen in 1900 and reedited by Louis Robert in 1977.[23] A letter from this emperor to Ephesus illustrates the relationships between Rome, Ephesus, and the wealthy benefactors of Ephesus. The text concerns the benefactions of Vedius

---

19. Vermeule, *Roman Imperial Art,* p. 232; cf. C. J. Hemer, "Unto the Angels of the Churches," *BH* 11 (1975): 19.

20. M. J. Price and B. L. Trell, *Coins and Their Cities* (Detroit: Wayne State University Press, 1977), p. 128; Magie, *Roman Rule,* vol. I, p. 619.

21. Price and Trell, *Coins and Their Cities,* p. 136.

22. E. L. Bowie, "The 'Temple of Hadrian' at Ephesus," *Zeitschrift für Papyrologie und Epigraphik* 8 (1971): 132–41.

23. Louis Robert, "Sur des inscriptions d'Éphèse," *Revue de Philologie*

Antoninus, who built the splendid gymnasium in the northern part of the city. Antoninus Pius writes:

> I learned of the generosity which Vedius Antoninus displays toward you not so much from your letters as from his. For wishing to obtain assistance from me for the decoration of the public buildings which he had promised to you, he revealed how many large buildings he is adding to the city. . . . I have granted his requests, and have noted that he prefers not to act in the usual way of politicians, who, to gain immediate applause, spend their benefactions on shows and distributions and prizes for games, but in a way in which he hopes to enhance the dignity of your city for the future.[24]

## Excavations

The great temple of Artemis, one of the seven wonders of the world, was razed by the Goths in the 3rd century. Over the centuries it was buried under 20 feet of alluvial soil, so that its very location was forgotten. With the influx of the Turks in the Middle Ages, Christianity was reduced to a minority faith. Writing in 1861, archbishop R. C. Trench described in melancholy terms the situation of the Turkish town of Selçuk, which had been established on the ruins of Ephesus:

> How awful for Ephesus the fulfilment of the threat (Rev. 2:5) has been, every modern traveller who has visited the ruins of that once famous city has borne witness. One who did so not long ago found only three Christians there, and these sunken in such ignorance and apathy as scarcely to have heard the names of St. Paul or St. John.[25]

Shortly after Trench penned these words, John Wood, an indefatigable British architect, began a six-year quest for the site of the Artemision. Wood finally discovered the foundations in 1869, and continued working at Ephesus

---

51 (1977): 7–14.

24. Cited in *A History of Rome Through the Fifth Century* II: *The Empire*, ed. A. H. M. Jones (New York: Harper & Row, 1970), p. 230.

25. R. C. Trench, *Commentary on the Epistles to the Seven Churches in Asia* (Minneapolis: Klock and Klock, 1978 reprint of 1897 edition), pp. 88–89.

until 1874. In 1904/1905 David G. Hogarth found a pit full of votive gifts, including jewelry and bronze and ivory statues of Artemis, which date to about 700 B.C.

The Austrians began their involvement at Ephesus with the work of W. Wilberg in 1894. Their excavations were continued until World War I, then resumed from 1926 to 1935. From 1954 to 1958 the work was directed by Franz Miltner. The Österreichischen Archäologischen Instituts has continued its activities until the present under the direction of W. Alzinger, H. Vetters, E. Fossel, V. M. Strocka, A. Bammer, and D. Knibbe.

## Monuments and Activities

To survey some of the major monuments of Ephesus, we need first to take note of three streets. The Arcadian Road, 530 meters (1740 feet) long and 11 meters (36 feet) wide, ran from the harbor east to the theater (figure 6, #9). The boulevard was originally flanked by columned halls, decorated with statues. The street in its present state dates from the rebuilding of the emperor Arcadius (395–408).

The eastern end of the Arcadian Road ran into Marble Street (#13), which ran south from the Artemision past the stadium and the theater (see photo VII.3).

From the southern end of Marble Street near the southeast corner of the commercial agora, Curetes Street ascends in a southeast direction (#19) between Mount Pion to the north and Mount Koressos to the south up to the civic agora (see figure 6, #22, and photo VII.4).

### The Civic Agora

Much of the recent effort of the Austrians has been concentrated on the Staatsmarkt or civic agora (see photo VII.5). It was here that a perpetual hearth was kept burning in the temple of Hestia (cf. Roman Vesta) Boulaia. Also located here were the *prytaneion* or town hall, and the semicircular *odeion* (#21), which served as a *bouleutērion* or council house (see photo VII.6). Most of the center as well as the eastern and southern borders remains unexcavated.

**VII.3**
The Marble Street runs from the base of Curetes Street north past the theater.

**VII.4**
Curetes Street runs from the southeast corner of the commercial agora up to the civic agora.

**VII.5**
The civic agora, where, in spite of recent excavations, much remains yet to be uncovered.

**VII.6**
The *odeion* in the civic agora functioned as a *bouleutērion,* that is, as a chamber for the city's council.

**VII.7**
The commercial agora was the area where the silversmiths sold their statues of Artemis.

## The Commercial Agora

The commercial agora, 110 meters (361 feet) square (#12), was built in Hellenistic times, and then enlarged under Augustus, Nero, and Caracalla (see photo VII.7). In the middle of it there once stood a sundial and a water clock.[26] It was in this area that the silversmiths who rioted in the nearby theater against Paul had their shops.[27]

## The Baths, Gymnasia, and Athletic Games

Ephesus was supplied with water from aqueducts which were built, as inscriptions inform us, under Augustus and Tiberius.[28] The great harbor gymnasium (#7), nearly completed by Domitian's reign, contained baths, as did the gymnasium erected in 150 by Publius Vedius Antoninus (#1). Recent work has concentrated on the Varius Baths (#23) in the civic agora, donated by the wealthy Ephesian sophist, Flavius Damianus.[29]

Ephesus was furnished with large gymnasia. To the east of the harbor gymnasium/bath was the Verulan Hall (#5), 200 by 240 meters (655 by 785 feet). This was a sports plaza which was decorated with thirteen kinds of marble by Claudius Verulanus, the high priest of Asia at the beginning of Hadrian's reign.[30]

In the north was the well-preserved Vedius gymnasium (#1) which even contained a swimming pool. The theater gymnasium (#6) has only been partially excavated.

The annual athletic games known as the Ephesia were first held as a pan-Ionian festival at the sanctuary of the

---

26. Keil, *Ephesos,* p. 54.

27. E. M. Blaiklock, *The Cities of the New Testament* (London: Pickering & Inglis, 1965), p. 67.

28. Vermeule, *Roman Imperial Art,* p. 465; G. M. A. Hanfmann, *From Croesus to Constantine* (Ann Arbor: University of Michigan Press, 1975), p. 48.

29. The same sophist gave funds for the poor, restored many public buildings, built a dining floor in the Artemision, and provided an elaborate portico between the Magnesian Gate and the Artemision to provide shelter from the rain. G. W. Bowersock, *Greek Sophists in the Roman Empire* (Oxford: Clarendon Press, 1969), p. 27.

30. Keil, *Ephesos,* pp. 80–81.

Panionion south of Ephesus on the Mycale promontory (figure 8). But in the early 4th century B.C. the games were transferred to Ephesus itself. The Ephesia included musical and dancing contests in which women also participated.[31] Women also played a prominent role in the festival known as the Artemisia.

During the reign of Vespasian a famous astrologer named Barbillus persuaded the emperor to sponsor a series of games known as the Barbillea (or Balbillea). The emperor Hadrian instituted games at Ephesus known as the Hadrianeia.[32]

Inscriptions record the generous donations of wealthy men who served either as gymnasiarchs or as *agōnothetai*, who presided over the games.[33] During the reign of Marcus Aurelius an Asiarch was given the honor and the burden of being *agōnothetēs* of the Hadrianeia for life.[34]

Other inscriptions commemorate the victories of athletes. A text dated to 300 B.C. celebrates the victory of an Athenodorus, who won a victory at the Panhellenic Nemean games in Greece.[35] The extraordinarily privileged position of athletes in the Greco-Roman world is indicated by a letter from Mark Antony written to the Assembly of Asia (either in 42/41 B.C. or 33/32 B.C.).

> On a former occasion also I was petitioned in Ephesus by Marcus Antonius Artemidorus, my friend and gymnastic trainer, along with the eponymous priest of the synod of sacred victors and crown-winners [ἱερονικῶν καὶ στεφανειτῶν] from the inhabited world, Charopinus of Ephesus, to ensure that the existing [privileges] of the synod should remain untouched, and to request, concern-

31. I. R. Arnold, "Festivals of Ephesus," *AJA* 76 (1972): 17–18.

32. Ibid., pp. 18–19; Millar, *The Emperor*, p. 449.

33. Jones, *Roman World*, p. 68; Louis Robert, "Sur des inscriptions d'Éphèse: fêtes, athlètes, empereurs, épigrammes," *Revue de Philologie* 41 (1967): 7–14.

34. Millar, *The Emperor*, p. 449.

35. Robert, "Inscriptions" (1967), pp. 14–32. For another boxer, see idem, *Opera Minora Selecta* (Amsterdam: A. M. Hakkert, 1969), vol. II, pp. 1138–41.

ing the other honours and privileges which they asked
from me, exemption from military service, from all litur-
gies, and from providing lodgings, as well as the rights of
truce, asylum and the wearing of the purple [πορφύρας] in
relation to the festival, that I should agree to write at once
to you.[36]

## Wild Beasts and Gladiators

In arguing for the reality of the resurrection, Paul
asked, "If I fought wild beasts in Ephesus for merely
human reasons, what have I gained?" (1 Cor. 15:32a,
NIV). Scholars have long debated whether this is a reference to an actual experience in the arena against wild
beasts or a metaphorical reference to Paul's opponents.
The latter is favored by W. Harold Mare in his recent
commentary.[37]

The *venatio* ("hunting") in which wild beasts were pitted
either against other beasts or against humans was popular
among the Romans. In the course of providing beasts for
these spectacles entire species such as the hippos of Nubia,
the elephants of North Africa, and the lions of Mesopotamia were exterminated.[38] The *venationes* were first introduced into Asia at Ephesus by Lucullus in 71/70 B.C.
"At Ephesus as many as 39 pairs took part in the course
of a thirteen-day celebration, and there were hunts at
Ephesus lasting five days during which 25 African beasts
were killed," according to I. R. Arnold.[39]

---

36. Cited in Millar, *The Emperor*, p. 456. For the Greek text, see R. K.
Sherk, *Roman Documents from the Greek East* (Baltimore: Johns Hopkins
University, 1969), p. 291.

37. W. Harold Mare, "1 Corinthians," in *The Expositor's Bible Commentary*, ed. F. E. Gaebelein (Grand Rapids: Zondervan, 1976), vol. X, p.
288. See also V. R. E. Osborn, "Paul and the Wild Beasts," *Journal of
Biblical Literature* 85 (1966): 225–30; A. J. Malherbe, "The Beasts at
Ephesus," *Journal of Biblical Literature* 87 (1968): 71–80; E. A. Judge,
"St. Paul and Classical Society," *Jahrbuch für Antike und Christentum* 15
(1972): 26.

38. George Jennison, *Animals for Show and Pleasure in Ancient Rome*
(Manchester: Manchester University Press, 1937); J. M. C. Toynbee,
*Animals in Roman Life and Art* (London: Thames and Hudson, 1973).

39. Arnold, "Festivals," p. 22.

The *ludi* or gladiatorial games originated in the Etruscan practice of sacrificing prisoners of war to the shades of their own fallen dead. In the Roman Republic it became customary for the *aediles* or "mayors" to sponsor such games out of their own funds to curry favor with the public.[40] Politicians such as the Asiarchs sponsored such games at Ephesus.[41]

With a few exceptions like Nero, the Romans had little taste for the nudity of the Greek athletic games. Conversely it was believed that the Greeks had little taste for the sanguinary gladiatorial games of the Romans. This impression has been conveyed by the fact that though the Roman intellectuals said almost nothing in protest against the games, Greek writers like Plutarch denounced them. Musonius and his student, Dio Chrysostom, both deplored the fact that the *ludi* were being sponsored in Greece.[42] In commenting upon an inscription from Smyrna C. J. Hemer remarks, "The popularity of this brutal Roman idea of sport in Smyrna is otherwise attested, though we do not usually associate such displays with the Greek East."[43]

The fact of the matter is that though the gladiatorial combats did not displace the Greek games, they became increasingly popular in Greece itself and in Asia Minor.[44] Many of the semicircular Greek theaters, even the famed theater of Dionysus at Athens, were remodeled as enclosed amphitheaters for the combats. Nero's stadium at Ephesus was thus transformed. Dio accused the Corinthians of watching these combats in some gully outside the city. The

40. M. Grant, *Gladiators* (New York: Delacorte, 1967); R. Auguet, *Cruelty and Civilization: The Roman Games* (London: George Allen and Unwin, 1972); A. Cameron, *Bread and Circuses* (London: King's College, 1974); J. Pearson, *Arena* (London: Thames and Hudson, 1973).

41. W. M. Ramsay, *The Cities and Bishoprics of Phrygia* (Oxford: Clarendon Press, 1895), vol. I, p. 76.

42. Jones, *Roman World*, p. 28.

43. Hemer, "Unto the Angels," *BH* 11 (1975): 66. Cf. Louis Robert, *Études Anatoliennes* (Amsterdam: A. M. Hakkert, 1970 reprint of the 1937 edition), pp. 138ff., for "inscriptions agonistiques" from Smyrna.

44. Barbara Levick, *Roman Colonies in Southern Asia Minor* (Oxford: Clarendon Press, 1967), p. 83.

old theater at Corinth was transformed into an amphitheater about the time of Jesus' birth.[45]

By a thorough study of the inscriptional data, especially from Asia Minor, Louis Robert has demonstrated the popularity of the gladiatorial games in the Greco-Roman cities.[46] Evidence for the Roman games has been found not only at Ephesus, but also at Miletus, Pergamum, Smyrna, Laodicea, and Hierapolis.[47]

Though denounced by Christian spokesmen, the barbaric games in which many believers were martyred maintained their popularity among the masses, as a celebrated passage in Augustine's *City of God* attests (c. 400). Gladiatorial games were finally stopped in 401 by the emperor Honorius, when a monk was killed as he tried to separate the fighters in the arena.[48] Games with animals continued until 681.

## The Theater

One of the first sites which the Austrians began to clear was the great theater (see photo VII.8), where twenty-four thousand screaming Ephesians gathered to protest Paul's ministry (Acts 19:23ff.). The theater, which was probably begun in the 2nd century B.C., was enlarged by Claudius. Nero erected the two-story stage building, to which a third story was added in the 2nd century A.D.[49]

The theater was embellished with numerous statues. An

---

45. Jones, *Roman World*, p. 32; J. Capps, "Observations on the Painted Venatio of the Theatre at Corinth and on the Arrangements of the Arena," *Hesperia Supplement* 8 (1949): 65.

46. Louis Robert, *Les Gladiateurs dans l'Orient Grec* (Amsterdam: A. M. Hakkert, 1971 reprint of the 1940 edition).

47. Magie, *Roman Rule*, vol. I, p. 655.

48. Grant, *Gladiators*, pp. 122–24; V. G. Ville, "Les jeux de gladiateurs dans l'empire chrétien," *Mélanges de l'école française de Rome* 62 (1960): 273–335.

49. Keil, *Ephesus*, pp. 88–89; E. Akurgal, *Ancient Civilizations and Ruins of Turkey*, 2nd ed. (Istanbul: Mobil Oil Türk A.S., 1970), p. 157; Daria de Bernardi Ferrero, *Teatri Classici in Asia Minore* III (Rome: "L'Erma" di Bretschneider, 1970), pp. 49–66.

inscription published in 1960 reports the donation of 120 statues of Cupids and of Nike (Victory).[50]

**VII.8**
The magnificent theater where twenty-four thousand shouting Ephesians met to protest Paul's ministry (Acts 19:23ff.).

## The Houses on the Slope

Recent work has concentrated on the Hanghäuser (#17), a series of *insulae* or houses on the slope of the hill south of Curetes Street. Beyond the front row of taverns and shops, the series of two-story apartments of upper-middle-class residences ascended the terraces. These dwellings were occupied from the 1st century A.D. to the 7th century (see photo VII.9).

The most interesting features of the houses are the wall paintings, including one of Socrates dated to the 1st century A.D. (see photo VII.10). The most stunning paintings

50. Louis Robert in Jean des Gagniers et al., *Laodicée du Lycos: Le Nymphée, Campagnes, 1961–1963* (Quebec: l'Université Laval, 1969), p. 258.

**VII.9**
Recent excavations on the slopes above Curetes Street have revealed finely decorated houses.

**VII.10**
In one of the houses on the slopes was uncovered this portrait of Socrates.

are theatrical scenes from Hanghaus 2, which date from the Severan period (early 3rd century).[51] These were discovered in 1967. On four panels there are four theatrical subjects with actors wearing dramatic masks. These are identified by inscriptions as depicting scenes from two of Euripides's plays and two of Menander's plays:

(1) Euripides's *Orestes*, lines 233–36, Orestes on a bed with Electra at his side.
(2) Euripides's *Iphigenia in Tauris*, lines 1159–1221. The badly damaged figures must represent Iphigenia before Thoas, king of Tauris.
(3) Menander's *Sicyonioi*, a fragment of which was newly published in 1964, depicting Dromon and Moschion.

51. H. Vetters, "Die Hanghäuser an der Kuretonstrasse," *Beiblatt* 50 (1972–75): 331–80; V. M. Strocka, "Wandmalerei," *Beiblatt* 50 (1972–75): 469–94; V. M. Strocka, *Die Wandmalerei der Hanghäuser in Ephesos* (Vienna: Österreichischen Akademie der Wissenschaften, 1977); see also a review of the latter by P. H. von Blanckenhagen in *AJA* 82 (1978): 565–67.

(4)  Menander's *Perikeiromene* ("Girl with Shorn Locks"), a
scene depicting two women and a man.[52]

Menander was the most popular writer of the Hellenistic
period. Of his more than a hundred plays, only one has
been preserved entire, the *Dyskolos* ("Bad-Tempered Man"),
which was recovered only in 1955.[53] Though the fact does
not prove that Paul attended the theater, he does quote
once from Menander's play *Thais* in 1 Corinthians 15:33:
"Bad company corrupts good character."[54]

## The Library of Celsus

Located at the western end of Curetes Street was the
magnificent Library of Celsus (#14). Two distinguished
citizens, father and son, are honored by the library. Most
scholars believe that the son, Gaius Julius Aquila, who was
consul suffectus in A.D. 110,[55] built the library in honor of
his father, Tiberius Julius Celsus Polemaeanus, consul suffectus in 92 and the proconsul of Asia in 105/106.[56] Other
scholars believe that the father may have begun the library. Celsus was given the unusual honor of burial under
the floor of the library. Three statues of Celsus and one of
his son were recovered.

The library was a relatively small building with a two-
story façade.[57] The main hall was 16.7 by 10.9 meters (55
by 36 feet). B. Götze estimated that the main level would

---

52.  V. M. Strocka, "Theaterbilder aus Ephesos," *Gymnasium* 80 (1973):
362–80, plates 16–20.

53.  T. B. L. Webster, *Hellenistic Poetry and Art* (New York: Barnes and
Noble, 1964), pp. 8–12; *Four Plays of Menander*, ed. E. Capps (Boston:
Ginn, 1910); *Theophrastus, The Characters; Menander, Plays and Fragments*
(Harmondsworth: Penguin, 1967).

54.  Paul makes but three other direct quotations from classical sources:
from Aratus (*Phaenomena* 5) and Ps.–Epimenides in Acts 17:28, and
from Epimenides *(De Oraculis)* in Titus 1:12. For possible allusions, see
E. B. Howell, "St. Paul and the Greek World," *Greece and Rome* 11
(1964): 7–29.

55.  Augustus reduced the term of the consul to a half year; the consul
suffectus was the consul for the second half of the year.

56.  Magie, *Roman Rule*, vol. I, p. 584; Hanfmann, *From Croesus to Constantine*, p. 43.

57.  Keil, *Ephesos*, pp. 105–06.

**VII.11**
The Library of Celsus (early 2nd century A.D.), at the foot of Curetes Street, is
being restored.

have stored about 4,000 rolls, and that an additional 5,500
rolls could have been stored in the second and third gal-
leries on shelves around the walls for a total of 9,500
rolls.[58] The Austrians, who have been restoring the library
since 1970 under Hermann Vetters, estimate that the
maximum capacity may have been as much as 12,000 rolls
(see photo VII.11).[59]

### The Auditorium

According to Acts 19:9 Paul "had discussions daily in the
lecture hall of Tyrannus" at Ephesus. The Western Text
adds the interesting gloss that Paul argued there "from the
fifth hour to the tenth," that is, from 11 a.m. to 4 p.m.

Ephesus was a noted center of rhetoric, particularly in
the period of the so-called Second Sophistic in the 2nd
century A.D.[60] Philostratus has Apollonius proclaiming
about the city:

58. B. Götze, "Antike Bibliotheken," *Jahrbuch der Deutschen Archäologischen Instituts* 52 (1937): 242.

59. W. Wilberg et al., *Ephesos: Die Bibliothek* (Vienna: Österreichisches
Archäologisches Institut, 1945); I. Hueber and V. M. Strocka, "Die
Bibliothek des Celsus," *Antike Welt* 6 (1975): 3–14.

60. Bowersock, *Greek Sophists*, p. 17.

But who will rob Ephesus of the chance to be cured? It is a city founded at the very origin of the race from the most sacred land of Attica; it has grown greater than all the cities of Ionia and Lydia; it has advanced to the sea, after outgrowing the land on which it was founded; it is a centre for philosophical and rhetorical studies, which make a city strong not in mere horses but in the abundance of its citizens, because it pursues wisdom. (*Life of Apollonius* VIII.8)[61]

A 1st-century A.D. Greek inscription found near the Library of Celsus contains the word αὐδειτώριον (from the Latin *auditorium*), which means the lecture hall for the recitations and speeches of professors, rhetors, and poets.[62] Hemer has suggested that the word may be nearly synonymous with the Greek word σχολή ("school") used in Acts 19:9, a word which originally meant "leisure."[63] A word in a letter of the empress Julia Domna contains a reference which is restored by Robert to read παιδ[αγωγεῖον] ("the school room").[64]

Unfortunately recent attempts to investigate the area east of the library have uncovered only late Byzantine walls and have failed to discover any remains of an auditorium.[65]

### The Brothel

North of Curetes Street behind the temple of Hadrian were some baths which were enlarged in about A.D. 400 by a Christian lady named Scholastica. In the block to the west, closer to the intersection with Marble Street, the excavators found some interesting rooms dating from the end of the 1st century or the beginning of the 2nd century. Closest to Curetes Street was a latrine, and behind it to the north a *tablinum* or dining room with a mosaic containing

---

61. Philostratus, *Life of Apollonius*, tr. C. P. Jones (Harmondsworth: Penguin, 1970), p. 217.
62. Keil, *Ephesos*, p. 109; Hueber and Strocka, "Die Bibliothek," p. 6.
63. C. J. Hemer, "Audeitorion," *TB* 24 (1973): 128.
64. Robert, "Inscriptions" (1967), p. 58.
65. H. Vetters, "Ephesos, 1976," *AS* 27 (1977): 39; M. J. Mellink, "Archaeology in Asia Minor," *AJA* 81 (1977): 308; 82 (1978): 327.

**VII.12** The "brothel" on Curetes Street.

four female heads representing the four seasons. A bath was located to the west of the *tablinum*.[66]

As an inscribed architrave block containing the word παιδισκήοις was found in the area of the latrine, Miltner interpreted the entire complex as a *paidiskeion* or brothel (see figure 6, #16, and photo VII.12). He suggested that the prostitutes, who lived upstairs, would dine with their customers and even bathe with them.

About 70 meters (230 feet) north on Marble Street a paving block surrounded by a railing has some symbols, which have been interpreted as erotic graffiti advertising the brothel. The symbols include a dotted triangle, a left foot, and a female figure with a five-towered coronet.[67] Hemer follows the popular interpretation by captioning a

66. F. Miltner, "Ephesus," *AS* 7 (1957): 27.

67. For an illustration see Hemer, "Unto the Angels," *BH* 11 (1975): 15. Hans Licht, *Sexual Life in Ancient Greece* (New York: Barnes & Noble, 1963 reprint of 1932 edition), p. 338, notes: "The shoe of such a street-walker has been accidentally preserved. On the sole of this shoe . . . the word AKOLOUTHI (that is, 'follow me') is nailed, so that, while the girl is walking along, the word is impressed on the soft ground of the street, and the passer-by can have no doubt as to her trade."

photo of these symbols: "In picture language it points customers to the brothel—a heart, girl and footsteps indicating the direction."[68] Some have interpreted the triangular symbol as the female pudenda.

Unfortunately for these spicy interpretations, a sober analysis of the evidence has raised doubts about the connection between the inscribed architrave found in the latrine and the so-called Freudenhaus or bordello north of it.[69] The popular interpretation of the paving block is quite clearly erroneous. As W. Jobst points out, the block is too far away, and moreover the symbols date from the 5th century A.D.[70] Furthermore, as Otto Meinardus points out, the left foot is a male foot, and the woman portrayed with a five-towered coronet is the goddess Tyche (Fortune).[71]

## The Artemision

The greatest structure at Ephesus was, of course, the Artemision or temple of Artemis (Roman Diana). The archaic temple was burned by fire in 356 B.C. according to tradition.[72] Excavators recently recovered part of an ivory statuette, which yielded a carbon-14 date of the mid-4th century B.C.: "It looks as if these archaic finds come from the levels of the burning due to Herostratos."[73]

---

68. Hemer, "Unto the Churches," *BH* 11 (1975): 15.

69. W. Jobst, "Das 'öffentliche Freudenhaus' in Ephesos," *Hauptblatt* 51 (1976–77): 61–69, 83.

70. Ibid., p. 67.

71. Otto F. A. Meinardus, "The Alleged Advertisement for the Ephesian Lupanar," *Wiener Studien,* n.F. 7 (1973): 244–49. There were probably bordellos in Ephesus; there were forty-five in Rome. Some of the rooms excavated at Pompeii were full of obscene graffiti and paintings, and were clearly used as brothels. See M. Grant, *Cities of Vesuvius* (London: Spring Books, 1971), p. 211.

72. For a general treatment of the Artemision, see D. G. Hogarth, *The Archaic Artemision* (London: British Museum, 1908); W. R. Lethaby, "The Earlier Temple of Artemis at Ephesus," *Journal of Hellenic Studies* 37 (1917): 1–16.

73. M. J. Mellink, "Archaeology in Asia Minor," *AJA* 79 (1975): 215; H. Vetters, "Ephesos, 1973," *AS* 24 (1974): 30.

**VII.13**
The site of the Artemision, the great temple of Artemis, which was one of the
Seven Wonders of the World. Only a single column stands amid the ruins.

The rebuilt temple was the largest structure in the Hellenistic world and the first of such monumental propor-
tions to be built entirely of marble. The temple was 110
meters (361 feet) long and 55 meters (180.5 feet) wide, set
on a platform 127 meters (420 feet) long and 73 meters
(240 feet) wide.[74] According to Pliny the Elder (*Natural
History* XXXVI.95ff.) there were 127 pillars of Parian
marble, 60 feet high, of which 36 were sculptured and
overlaid with gold.[75] Only a solitary standing column
amidst fragments may be seen in situ (see photo VII.13).
One of the sculptured drums is on display in the British
Museum.[76] The capitals were of the Ionic order, and the
columns were distributed in a dipteral style with eight columns on the main façade.

Many of the architectural details are preserved for us on

---

74. Keil, *Ephesos*, p. 49. The figures cited by Robert H. Mounce, *The
Book of Revelation* (Grand Rapids: Wm. B. Eerdmans, 1977), p. 86, refer
to the terrace and not to the temple proper.

75. Anton Bammer, *Die Architektur des jüngeren Artemision von Ephesos*
(Wiesbaden: F. Steiner, 1972), p. 21.

76. Akurgal, *Ancient Civilizations*, p. 150. Hanfmann, *From Croesus to
Constantine*, p. 13, comments: "Unfortunately less than one percent of
the sculptures of the Artemision remains and these are mostly in small
fragments."

coins dating from the reign of Claudius to Valerian.[77] According to M. J. Price and B. L. Trell, a recently discovered coin of Maximus preserves "one of the most exciting views of the great temple":

> Three windows figure prominently [in the pediment] and in addition there are four statues. . . . These may have been the famous Amazons which decorated the 5th century B.C. altar and which may have been moved to the pediment of the 4th century temple in the rebuilding.[78]

### The Altar

In 1965 the Austrian excavators made a spectacular discovery before the western façade of the temple: they found the great altar. Although their excavations were complicated by the high water table, they discovered that in the late archaic period (c. 450 B.C.), a U-shaped wall was interposed between the altar and the temple with the open side to the sea (see figure 7). The altar stood in an area 39.7 by 20.7 meters (130 by 68 feet), provided with drainage canals.[79] Among the items which were found around the altar were fragments of statues (including a magnificent horse's head), ivory objects, and a crystal which may have been used for divinatory purposes.[80]

As Anton Bammer reconstructs the situation, the priest stood on the ramp approaching the large sacrificial altar, and made his offerings while facing south toward a cult statue.[81] On the basis of numismatic evidence, Price and Trell believe that there were windows in the west pediment: "We can now visualize the people assembled before

77. On the general subject, see B. L. Trell, *The Temple of Artemis at Ephesos* (New York: American Numismatic Society, 1945).

78. Price and Trell, *Coins and Their Cities,* pp. 120, 126–27.

79. M. J. Mellink, "Archaeology in Asia Minor," *AJA* 73 (1969): 221; Anton Bammer, "Recent Excavations at the Altar of Artemis in Ephesus," *Arch* 27.3 (1974): 202–05; idem, "Wo einst ein Weltwunder stand," *Das Altertum* 21 (1975): 27–35.

80. Bammer, *Die Architektur,* p. 56; R. Fleischer, "Skulpturenfunde — Ephesos (1960–69/70)," *Beiblatt* 50 (1972–75): 461–68.

81. Bammer, *Die Architektur,* p. 7; idem, "Die Entwicklung des Opferkultes am Altar des Artemis von Ephesos," *IM* 23/24 (1973–74): 53–63.

*Figure 7*

**TEMPLE AND ALTAR AT EPHESUS**

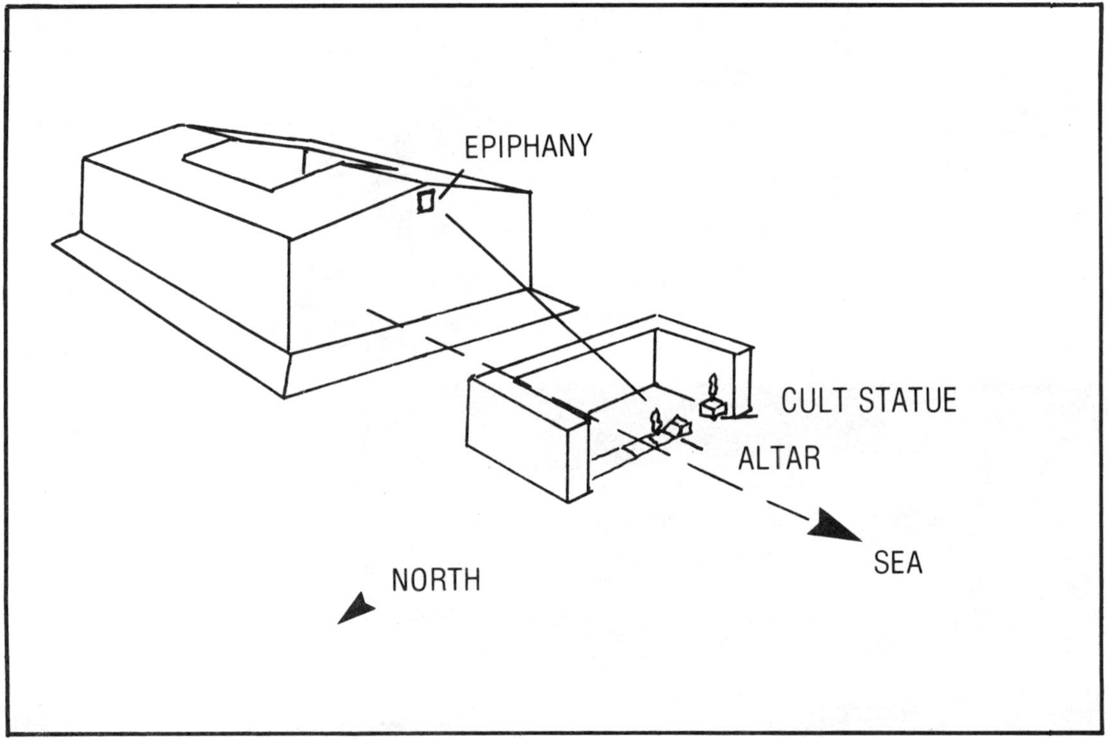

EPIPHANY

CULT STATUE

ALTAR

SEA

NORTH

the temple waiting for the epiphany of the goddess or a symbol of her divinity in the windows."[82]

**VII.14**
A statue of Artemis of Ephesus.

*The Statues of Artemis*

Coins also depict the cult statue of the goddess within the sanctuary with such precision that one can even make out her stag.[83] Numerous statues of the Artemis of Ephesus have been recovered from Ephesus and from sites as far away as Caesarea in Palestine. Two fine marble examples are found in the Seljuk Museum (see photo VII.14).

From 150 B.C. the goddess is depicted with numerous rows of bulbous objects on her chest which are commonly interpreted as breasts. Various other interpretations have been suggested. Ramsay thought that they were bee eggs, and A. Wotschitzky that they were ostrich eggs, which were symbols of fertility.[84] After reviewing all the alternatives, Robert Fleischer comes to the conclusion that no explanation is really satis-

---

82. Price and Trell, *Coins and Their Cities*, p. 131. A coin of Macrinus depicts the altar of the imperial temple, and worshipers by it. See ibid., p. 211.

83. B. L. Trell, "Architecture on Ancient Coins," *Arch* 29 (1976): 9. See the front cover of the issue.

84. A. Wotschitzky, "Ephesus: Past, Present and Future of a Great Metropolis," *Arch* 14 (1961): 209.

factory.[85] Elma Heinzel believes that the ornamented garment of the goddess depicted not just fertility motifs but astrological symbols.[86]

The intense devotion given to the goddess has been underscored by an inscription (dated 350–300 B.C.) which records that forty-five inhabitants of Sardis were condemned to die as they had maltreated a sacred embassy from Ephesus bearing cloaks for the statue of Artemis.[87]

The riot against Paul was instigated by Demetrius and the silversmiths, who made their wealth by selling silver statues of Artemis. When the pagans were converted, they stopped coming to the temple and sales fell off. An inscription in Greek and Latin records that Gaius Vibius Salutaris in A.D. 104 donated thirty-one gold and silver statuettes, including some of Artemis, to be set up in the theater.[88]

*The Temple as Bank and Asylum*

Not only was there a great deal of profit involved in the business of catering to the pilgrim traffic, there was enormous wealth deposited in the temple itself, which functioned as a kind of treasury or bank. As early as the 5th century B.C. deposits were received on account, and money was loaned out. According to Dio Chrysostom (XXXI.54):

> You know about the Ephesians, of course, and that large sums of money are in their hands, some of it belonging to private citizens and deposited in the temple of Artemis, not alone money of the Ephesians but also of aliens and of

85. Robert Fleischer, *Artemis von Ephesos und Verwandte Kultstatuen aus Anatolien und Syrien* (Leiden: E. J. Brill, 1973), pp. 73–85. For a review, see M. J. Mellink, *AJA* 79 (1975): 107–08.

86. Elma Heinzel, "Zum Kult der Artemis von Ephesos," *Hauptblatt* 50 (1972–73): 243–51.

87. F. Sokolowski, "A New Testimony on the Cult of Artemis of Ephesus," *Harvard Theological Review* 58 (1965): 427–31.

88. Magie, *Roman Rule*, vol. I, p. 583; Adolf Deissmann, *Light from the Ancient East* (Grand Rapids: Baker, 1965 reprint of 1922 edition), p. 113; Richard Oster, "The Ephesian Artemis as an Opponent of Early Christianity," *Jahrbuch für Antike und Christentum* 19 (1976): 24–44.

persons from all parts of the world, and in some cases of commonwealths and kings, money which all deposit there in order that it may be safe, since no one has ever yet dared to violate that place, although countless wars have occurred in the past and the city has often been captured.[89]

During the Civil War between Pompey and Caesar, Pompey had ordered Scipio to seize the funds from the temple, but this was not done as Caesar moved too quickly (Caesar, *Civil Wars* III.33). In spite of Dio's claim that the funds were sacrosanct, they were loaned out at interest according to Nicolaus of Damascus (fragment 65), and were a constant source of temptation.

Shortly before Paul's arrival, the proconsul Paulus Fabius Persicus passed a decree regulating the finances of the temple, abolishing the sale of priesthoods, and reducing the personnel maintained on temple funds.[90]

Another aspect of the sanctuary that was liable to abuse was the right of sanctuary within the temple's precincts. According to Strabo, Alexander extended the precinct around the Artemision to a stade (200 meters or 656 feet). Mithradates extended it further, and Mark Antony then doubled it. This extension proved attractive to evildoers who sought refuge in the area, so that Augustus revoked the enlargement authorized by Antony.[91]

## Neōkoros

The town clerk, who was the chief executive officer of the city, reminded the angry Ephesian mob that their city was a *neōkoros* ("temple keeper"; KJV, "worshipper") of the great goddess (Acts 19:35). As we have seen, the Greek word originally meant "temple sweeper" but came to have the honorific meaning of "warden."

---

89. See Jones, *Roman World,* p. 30. A bilingual inscription, published in 1960, records that Artemis was granted revenues from certain sacred lands. See Millar, *The Emperor,* p. 448.

90. F. Millar, ed., *The Roman Empire and Its Neighbours* (London: Weidenfeld & Nicolson, 1970), p. 199.

91. Millar, *The Emperor,* p. 448; Magie, *Roman Rule,* vol. I, p. 470.

In the later imperial period the title was awarded to cities in honor of temples expressly designated for the worship of the emperor. There has been a long-standing controversy as to whether the neocorate temples were founded by the city or by the province of Asia. Ramsay favored the former position.[92] The publication of recent inscriptions has convinced Robert that the latter must have been the case.[93]

## The Asiarchs

During his ministry at Ephesus Paul must have contacted the highest levels of society, for we read that "certain of the chief of Asia, which were his friends" (Acts 19:31, KJV) tried to dissuade Paul from endangering his life by going to the theater. These men were Asiarchs.

The available evidence suggests that these Asiarchs were the high priests of the Asian *Koinon* or Assembly.[94] Known also as *sebastophantes,* these influential Roman citizens presided over the imperial cult. One high priest was probably elected from each of the various Asian cities on a rotating annual basis.[95] It was the most prestigious office in the province of Asia to which one could aspire.

It is quite clear that these officials were chosen from the wealthiest men of the cities. They were greatly honored and were quite conspicuously dressed. Dio Chrysostom declares:

> I refer to the "blessed ones," who exercise authority over all your priests, whose title represents one of the two continents in its entirety [i.e., Asiarch]. For these men too owe

92. Ramsay, *The Cities and Bishoprics,* vol. I, p. 58.

93. Robert, "Inscriptions" (1967), p. 48.

94. C. A. Behr, *Aelius Aristides and the Sacred Tales* (Amsterdam: A. M. Hakkert, 1968), p. 65; Jones, *Roman World,* p. 69; G. W. Bowersock, *Augustus and the Greek World* (Oxford: Clarendon Press, 1965), p. 117.

95. W. M. Ramsay, *The Social Basis of Roman Power in Asia Minor* (Amsterdam: A. M. Hakkert, 1967), pp. 13, 34, cites inscriptions from Phocaea and from Acmonia, both before A.D. 129. See Behr, *Aelius Aristides,* p. 63; Lily Ross Taylor, "The Asiarchs," in F. J. Foakes Jackson and Kirsopp Lake, eds., *The Beginnings of Christianity: The Acts of the Apostles; V. Additional Notes* (Grand Rapids: Baker, 1966 reprint of 1932 edition), p. 261.

their "blessedness" to crowns and purple and a throng of long-haired lads bearing frankincense. (XXXV.10)

These priests wore unusually ornate crowns adorned with miniature busts of the imperial family, and were given the title *stephanophorus*.[96]

But just as there were great honors there were also obligations which were both time-consuming and expensive. The high priest was expected to undertake numerous projects for the city and the province, such as the sponsorship of gladiatorial combats and animal contests.[97] For this reason and because of his chronic illnesses, Aelius Aristides refused to accept nomination to this office and to other such posts, in spite of repeated efforts to elect him.[98]

### Jews at Ephesus

Among the very sparse evidences of the Jews at Ephesus are some inscriptions, including a funerary monument of M. Aurelius Moussios which was prepared by the Jews at the public expense of the community.[99]

Meinardus also notes a menorah carved into the steps leading to the Library of Celsus. Several terra-cotta lamps with the menorah design and a unique glass with the menorah, shofar, and lulab were found in the Cemetery of the Seven Sleepers.[100]

---

96. Ramsay, *The Cities and Bishoprics,* vol. I, p. 56; Jones, *Roman World,* p. 69.

97. The people of Smyrna urged the Asiarch Philippos to loose a lion upon Polycarp. When he refused, Polycarp was burned to death.

98. Behr, *Aelius Aristides,* pp. 64–65; Bowersock, *Greek Sophists,* p. 37.

99. S. Safrai and M. Stern, eds., *The Jewish People in the First Century* (Philadelphia: Fortress Press, 1974), p. 483.

100. Otto F. A. Meinardus, *St. John of Patmos and the Seven Churches of the Apocalypse* (Athens: Lycabettus, 1974), p. 37; idem, "The Christian Remains of the Seven Churches of the Apocalypse," *BA* 37 (1974): 71.

The Grotto of the Seven Sleepers is located at the foot of Mount Pion. It commemorates the legend that seven young princes slept for almost two hundred years to escape the Decian persecutions (250). Theodosius II (408–50) built a church to enshrine the cave, which became one of the most popular sites for pilgrims during the Middle Ages. The site was excavated in 1927–28.

## Christians at Ephesus

### St. Paul

It is remarkable that there is almost nothing at Ephesus to remind us of the great apostle whose ministry made the city so memorable in the history of Christianity. The so-called Prison of St. Paul shown to tourists at the western end of Mount Koressos near the entrance to the ancient port is but part of the wall built by Lysimachus.[101]

In 1955, in a cavelike chapel on Mount Koressos south of the city, graffiti were found which are evidence that Paul was invoked as a saint at Ephesus.[102]

### St. John

The Church of St. John is located on a hilltop 3 miles from the ruins of the city, overlooking the site of the Artemision.[103] By the 2nd century a small church marked the tomb of St. John. This was replaced in the 4th century by the so-called Theodosian basilica.

In the 6th century Justinian (527–65) erected at the site "the greatest and most magnificent church of early Christendom" (see photo VII.15). The church was 120 meters (394 feet) long and 40 meters (131 feet) wide, with six large domes over the center aisle and five small domes covering the narthex.[104] As dust from St. John's tomb was believed to have healing properties, the church became one of the most popular shrines for pilgrims during the Middle Ages (see photo VII.16).

Excavations conducted from 1927 to 1929 laid bare the crypt of St. John. The church, which may have taken thirty-five years to build originally, is being restored.[105]

---

101. Otto F. A. Meinardus, *St. Paul in Ephesus and the Cities of Galatia and Cyprus* (Athens: Lycabettus, 1973), pp. 84–85.

102. D. Boyd, "Ephesus," *IDBS,* p. 270.

103. Akurgal, *Ancient Civilizations,* pp. 144ff.; Meinardus, *St. John of Patmos,* pp. 50, 55–57; idem, "The Christian Remains," p. 73.

104. Keil, *Ephesos,* pp. 36–38.

105. H. Vetters, "Ephesos, 1972," *AS* 23 (1973): 36. See H. Plommer, "St. John's Church, Ephesus," *AS* 12 (1962): 119–30. On traditions about John, see F. F. Bruce, "St. John at Ephesus," *Bulletin of the John Rylands Library* 60 (1977–78): 339–61.

**VII.15** The Church of St. John, built by Justinian (6th century A.D.).

**VII.16** The "Tomb of St. John" was a popular goal of pilgrims.

## The Virgin Mary

By the 4th century apocryphal works such as *The Assumption of Mary* were being composed. The Dormition Abbey on Mount Zion in Jerusalem commemorated the site where the Virgin allegedly died, and the Tomb of the Virgin in the Kidron Valley marked the place where her body was laid.[106] In 1950 Pius XII stated that the Assumption of the Virgin was a dogma of Catholicism.

A rival tradition had developed by the 4th century that St. John had taken the Virgin with him to Ephesus (cf. John 19:27). But, as Ramsay notes, there were those who questioned such a tradition:

> Epiphanius [bishop of Cyprus] about A.D. 375 remarks that the Scriptures say nothing about the death of the Virgin, whether she died or not, whether she was buried or not, and that in the Scriptures there is no authority for the opinion that when John went away into (the Province) Asia, he took her with him.[107]

The third ecumenical council, which was held at Ephesus in 431, established the Virgin as *theotokos* ("mother of God") and condemned Nestorius of Constantinople.[108] It is probable that the council met at the so-called Church of the Virgin Mary (figure 6, #4), a double building 800 feet long, which had earlier functioned as a kind of stock exchange.[109]

In the early 19th century a nun in Germany had visions of a house in Ephesus that she believed was the house of

---

106. Eugene Hoade, *Guide to the Holy Land*, 4th ed. (Jerusalem: Franciscan, 1962), pp. 223–26. The tomb was examined in 1956. The rock slab had been chipped by pilgrims who took away "de petra sepulchri mariae" as relics.

107. W. M. Ramsay, *Pauline and Other Studies in Early Christian History* (London: Hodder & Stoughton, 1906), p. 144. Chapter 5 deals with "The Worship of the Virgin Mary at Ephesus."

108. Hubert Jedin, *Ecumenical Councils in the Catholic Church* (New York: Herder and Herder, 1960), pp. 28–36.

109. Meinardus, "The Christian Remains," p. 73.

the Virgin. Some fifty years later, a priest from Smyrna found a house on Mount Solemissos, south of Ephesus, which seemed to fit her description. In 1914 the pope declared that this house was a sacred site for pilgrims.[110]

110.  Ibid., p. 74; S. Perowne, *The Journeys of St. Paul* (London: Hamlyn, 1973), p. 76.

# 8

## MILETUS

### Location

The great Ionian city of Miletus was situated on the
south shore of the Gulf of Latmos on a peninsula east of
the island of Lade (see figure 8). On the north shore of the
gulf was the estuary of the Meander River. The deposition
of silt at the river's mouth was so great that eventually the
gulf was filled in, transforming a portion of the gulf into
Lake Bafa and attaching the island of Lade to the coast.

Miletus was no longer on the coast by the 4th century
A.D.[1] The land has been built up at the rate of about 600
meters (2,000 feet) a century, so that the ruins of Miletus
are now located at Yeni-Balat some 5 miles from the coast.

Miletus once had four harbors. The oldest of these was a
bay west of the peninsula near the theater (figure 9, #2).
The main port was known as the Lion Harbor as it was
flanked by two marble lions, whose damaged torsos may
still be seen in situ. This haven could be closed off with
chains (figure 9, #1). At the south end of this harbor

---

1. Adelaide G. Dunham, *The History of Miletus* (London: University of
London Press, 1915), p. 4.

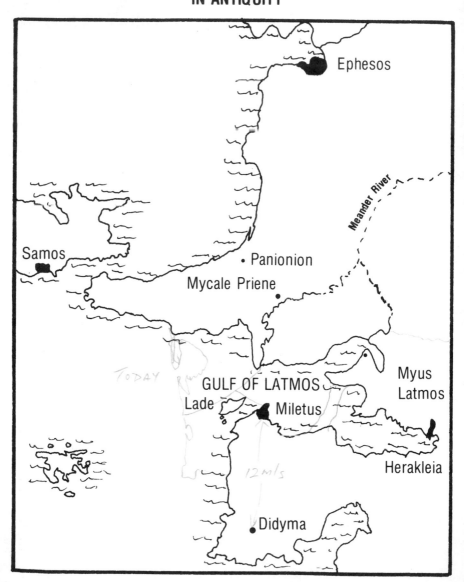

*Figure 8*    **THE MOUTH OF THE MEANDER
IN ANTIQUITY**

Ephesos

Meander River

Samos

Panionion

Mycale Priene

TODAY

GULF OF LATMOS

Myus
Latmos

Lade    Miletus

Herakleia

12 m/s

Didyma

# TODAY

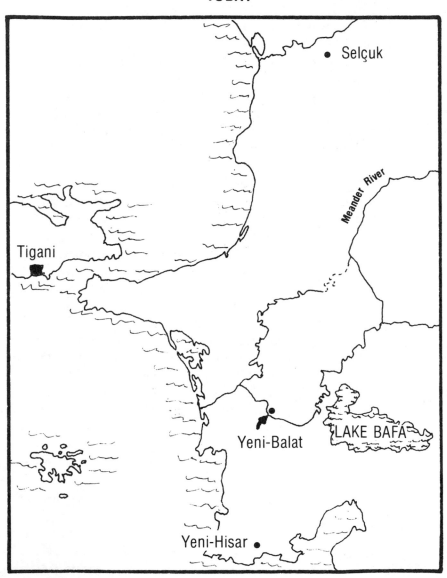

After Gerhard Kleiner, *Die Ruinen von Milet* (Berlin: W. de Gruyter, 1968)

stands the round base of a large monument, which was
probably erected by Augustus to commemorate his victory
over Antony and Cleopatra at Actium in 31 B.C.

## New Testament References

On his way back to Jerusalem from the third missionary
journey, Paul passed by Ephesus and landed at Miletus, no
doubt at the Lion Harbor. He then called for the elders of
Ephesus to meet with him at Miletus (Acts 20:15–17). In
his last letter Paul mentions that he left the sick Trophimus
at Miletus (2 Tim. 4:20). Such sparse references little be-
tray the importance of this city which played a key role in
Greek history.

## Historical Background

From archaeological evidence recovered from the area
of the temple of Athena (figure 9, #12), we know that a
Minoan colony was superseded by the Mycenaeans about
the 13th century B.C.[2] Hittite texts from the periods of the
Trojan War refer to the *Ahhiyawa* (Achaeans) at *Milawanda*
(Miletus).[3] But according to the *Iliad* (II.868–69), the Car-
ians of Miletus were engaged against the Greeks at Troy.

When the Dorians overran Mycenaean Greece in the
12th century B.C., a stream of refugees settled on the west
coast of Asia Minor, chiefly in the area of Ionia. During
the archaic period (8th–6th centuries B.C.), Miletus became the foremost colonizer of the Black Sea region,
founding ninety cities there according to Pliny the Elder.
Milesian intellectuals including the geographer/historian
Hecataeus and the philosophers Thales, Anaximander,
and Anaximenes led the Greek world in the renaissance of
the 6th century B.C. Ironically, as Henri Metzger points
out, the period of Miletus's greatest glory has not been
greatly illuminated by the excavations:

2.  Gerhard Kleiner, *Alt-Milet* (Wiesbaden: F. Steiner, 1966).
3.  D. L. Page, *History and the Homeric Iliad* (Berkeley: University of
California Press, 1959), p. 281; George L. Huxley, *Achaeans and Hittites*
(Belfast: Queen's University Press, 1960).

We have already noted that, paradoxically, the archaeology of Miletus has made most progress in the oldest periods but has told us nothing about the city of the 7th and 6th centuries, the importance of which is attested by the historical and literary sources.[4]

Together with other Ionian cities Miletus fell under Persian hegemony soon after Cyrus captured Lydia. The Milesian tyrants, Histiaeus and Aristagoras, instigated the Ionian Revolt against the Persians in 499 B.C. The Greeks were finally defeated off the coast of Lade in 494 by the Persians, who took harsh revenge against Miletus and its sanctuary at Didyma (Herodotus VI.20). It has been only recently near the Delphinion (figure 9, #3) that evidence of the Persian destruction has been brought to light.[5] In 479 the Athenians and the Spartans landed at Mycale (figure 8) to liberate the Ionians from the Persians, reputedly on the same day as the battle of Plataea in Greece.

The devastated city was rebuilt on the gridiron plan by Hippodamus, the famous city-planner from Miletus.[6] Because of the progressive silting-in of the bay, Miletus declined in importance in the Hellenistic era.

In the early Roman period Miletus vied for the honor of erecting a temple to Tiberius; it was passed over in favor of Smyrna. C. C. Vermeule comments that Miletus has yielded surprisingly few Julio-Claudian monuments. We have an inscription in honor of Augustus, a text from Claudius to followers of Dionysus, and an inscription from a temple which Caligula had built for worship of himself.[7]

In the 2nd century Miletus became the beneficiary of numerous imperial benefactions. Trajan paid for canals,

---

4. Henri Metzger, *Anatolia* II (London: Cresset, 1969), p. 103.

5. M. J. Mellink, "Archaeology in Asia Minor," *AJA* 78 (1974): 123. The fact that Miletus provided eighty triremes for the battle of Lade indicates that the city's population at this time was about one hundred thousand.

6. James McCredie, "Hippodamos of Miletos," in *Studies Presented to George M. A. Hanfmann*, ed. D. G. Mitten, J. G. Pedley, and J. A. Scott (Mainz: P. von Zabern, 1972), pp. 95–100.

7. C. C. Vermeule, *Roman Imperial Art in Greece and Asia Minor* (Cambridge: Harvard University Press, 1968), pp. 219, 463.

aqueducts, and above all for the construction of the Sacred Way (see p. 126). Three altars dedicated to Hadrian have been recovered. Faustina, the wife of Marcus Aurelius, was honored with the erection of sumptuous baths (see p. 122). A bilingual letter of Marcus Aurelius was found in 1971 in the Sacred Way near the nymphaeum.[8]

## Excavations

German scholars under the leadership of Theodor Wiegand investigated Miletus from 1899 to 1914. Further work was conducted in 1938-39, and since 1955 under Carl Weickert, Rudolf Naumann, and G. Kleiner. An earthquake that destroyed the village of Yeni-Balat in 1955 enabled the Germans to investigate further areas.[9] A new museum has been erected near the ruins.[10]

## The Markets

Miletus possessed three outstanding agoras or markets: (1) The oldest market was the North Agora (figure 9, #4), which contained a stoa 160 meters (525 feet) long. There were thirty shops, which were built in the Hellenistic period.[11] (2) The West Agora (#10) was built in the late Hellenistic period. (3) The grandest market of all was the South Agora (#6), which was the largest of all Greek markets, measuring 164 by 196 meters (525 by 645 feet) and covering 8 acres. Its east hall was known as the "stadium stoa" because it was a stade (200 meters) long. Built under Antiochus I in the 3rd century B.C., the agora had

---

8. M. J. Mellink, "Archaeology in Asia Minor," *AJA* 76 (1972): 182; P. Herrmann, "Eine Kaiserkunde der Zeit Marc Aurels aus Milet," *IM* 25 (1975): 149–66.

9. J. P. Lewis, "Following Paul with Hertz," *Restoration Quarterly* 15 (1972): 132.

10. For the more recent references to the excavations, see W. Real, "Bibliographie der bisherigen Forschungen über Milet, Stand 1974," *IM* 25 (1975): 259–66.

11. E. Akurgal, *Ancient Civilizations and Ruins of Turkey*, 2nd ed. (Istanbul: Mobil Oil Türk A.S., 1970), p. 215.

**VIII.1** The *bouleutērion* or council chamber could hold 1,500.

**VIII.2**
The theater. The two columns supported an awning which shaded Faustina, the wife of Marcus Aurelius, upon her visit in A.D. 164. An inscription in the fifth row indicated reserved seats for "the Jews, who are also called God-fearing."

seventy-eight triple-chambered stores.[12] The two-story
north gate (#8), constructed in 165 B.C., has been rebuilt
for display in the Pergamum Museum in Berlin.

The Milesians were famous for their furniture, carpets,
and woolen cloths. A recently published price catalogue of
the 3rd century A.D. lists the price of double-dyed Milesian purple wool of the best quality as between ten and
twelve thousand denarii per pound.[13]

## The Council Chamber

The *bouleutērion* or council chamber (figure 9, #5) between the North and the South Agora is one of the most
important buildings at Miletus.[14] Inscriptions indicate that
it was established by Antiochus IV (175–64 B.C.). R. E.
Wycherley observes, "The Council-House of Miletus was
the most stately of its kind, and by reason of the size of the
chamber the most remarkable in construction."[15]

The council chamber was approached by a propylon,
which led into a large colonnaded courtyard. The auditorium proper, 23 by 35 meters (75 by 115 feet), contained a semicircular arrangement of seats which could
hold 1,500 (see photo VIII.1). The thirty inscriptions
which have been recovered from the site span the period
from the 2nd century B.C. to the 3rd century A.D.[16]

## The Baths and the Nymphaeum

To the east of the North Agora, Cn. Vergilius Capito,
proconsul of Asia, erected some splendid baths. To the

12. G. M. A. Hanfmann, *From Croesus to Constantine* (Ann Arbor: University of Michigan Press, 1975), p. 215.
13. P. Herrmann, "Milesischer Purpur," *IM* 25 (1975): 141–47.
14. Gerhard Kleiner, *Die Ruinen von Milet* (Berlin: W. de Gruyter,
1968), pp. 77–88.
15. R. E. Wycherley, *How the Greeks Built Cities* (London: Macmillan,
1962), p. 132.
16. K. Tuchelt, "Bouleuterion und Ara Augusti," *IM* 25 (1975): 91–
113.

west of the South Agora the great Baths of Faustina were built (#9), equipped with a swimming pool.[17]

The nymphaeum (nymphaion) was a monumental three-story fountain just north of the northeast corner of the South Agora. The elaborate building, the ground floor of which is still intact, was erected by Trajan.[18]

### The Gymnasia and the Stadium

South of the Baths of Capito was a large gymnasium donated by the Pergamene king, Eumenes II. It contained a propylon, a palaestra, and five rooms for lectures and study.[19] To the west of the Baths of Faustina was a huge palaestra, about 79 meters (260 feet) square.

The great stadium south of the Theater Harbor (figure 9, #11) was also a gift of Eumenes II. It was 191 meters (627 feet) long and 29.5 meters (97 feet) wide. The unusual stadium, which had no rounded end, could hold fifteen thousand spectators.

### The Theater

The theater (figure 9, #2) was first begun in the 4th century B.C. on a hill over 30 meters (98 feet) high overlooking the Theater Harbor. With a frontage of 140 meters (460 feet), the large theater could accommodate fifteen thousand. Two of the four columns of the imperial baldachin, erected for the visit of Faustina in A.D. 164, are still to be seen in situ (see photo VIII.2).[20]

An inscription from Miletus records that the emperor Claudius in 48 wrote "to the sacred victors and performers devoted to Dionysus" to assure the actors that he would not only preserve their rights and privileges but would try

17. Kleiner, *Die Ruinen,* pp. 104–05; G. Kleiner, *Das römische Milet* (Wiesbaden: F. Steiner, 1970), pp. 16–19. There was a similar swimming pool in the gymnasium at Sardis. See G. M. A. Hanfmann, "The Sixteenth Campaign at Sardis (1973)," *Bulletin of the American Schools of Oriental Research* 215 (1974): 46, 50–51.

18. Kleiner, *Die Ruinen,* pp. 116–17.

19. Ibid., p. 89.

20. Ibid., pp. 68–76; Kleiner, *Das römische Milet,* p. 20; Akurgal, *Ancient Civilizations,* p. 207; Daria de Bernardi Ferrero, *Teatri Classici in Asia Minore* III (Rome: "L'Erma" di Bretschneider, 1970), pp. 86–95.

*Figure 9*　　　　　# PLAN OF MILETUS

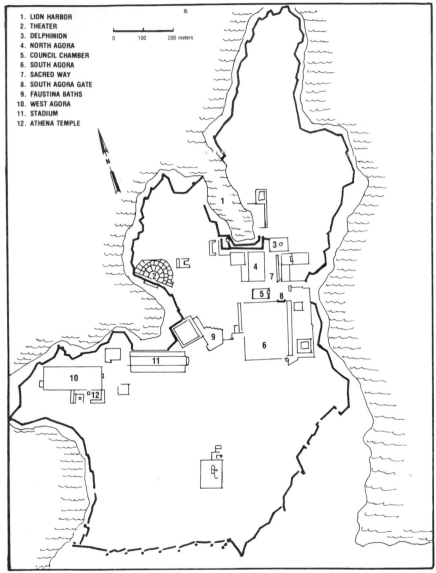

1. LION HARBOR
2. THEATER
3. DELPHINION
4. NORTH AGORA
5. COUNCIL CHAMBER
6. SOUTH AGORA
7. SACRED WAY
8. SOUTH AGORA GATE
9. FAUSTINA BATHS
10. WEST AGORA
11. STADIUM
12. ATHENA TEMPLE

0    100    200 meters

After Gerhard Kleiner, *Das Römische Milet* (Wiesbaden: F. Steiner, 1970)

to increase them.[21] Another inscription from the reign of Commodus celebrates the victory of a lyre player at a contest at Didyma.[22]

## The Jews and the Synagogue

According to Josephus *(Antiquities* XIV.244–46) the Romans, perhaps as early as the 1st century B.C., had intervened at Miletus to guarantee the Jews their right to observe the Sabbath, and "perform their other rites in accordance with their native laws."

In the fifth row of the theater is a remarkable inscription, τόπος Εἰουδέων τῶν καὶ Θεοσεβίον, which Adolf Deissmann rendered, "place of the Jews, who also are called God-fearing."[23] That is, he interpreted the epithet *theosebion* as referring to the Jews. But in the New Testament the related word *sebomenos,* as in Acts 13:43; 17:4, 17, for example, refers to Gentile proselytes to Judaism (cf. also *phoboumenos* in Acts 13:16, 26). H. Hommel concludes that the inscription refers not to the Jews proper, nor to Jews *and* proselytes, but to proselytes who were known to other Gentiles as "Jews."[24]

Recently at Aphrodisias in southwest Turkey a long inscription was discovered which contains "lists of the members of the local synagogue, and along with them, the names of a group described as *theosebeis.* . . . "[25] The text also refers to the members of the synagogue by occupation as fullers, coppersmiths, a goldsmith, and a sausagemaker.

Just by the southwest corner of the Lion Harbor was a synagogue in the form of a basilica with a nave flanked by

21. Fergus Millar, *The Emperor in the Roman World* (London: Duckworth, 1977), p. 459.

22. T. Pekáry, "Inschriftenfunde aus Milet 1959," *IM* 15 (1965): 121–23.

23. Adolf Deissmann, *Light from the Ancient East* (Grand Rapids: Baker, 1965 reprint of the 1922 edition), p. 451.

24. H. Hommel, "Juden und Christen im kaiserzeitlichen Milet; Überlegungen zur Theaterinschrift," *IM* 25 (1975): 167–95.

25. M. J. Mellink, "Archaeology in Asia Minor," *AJA* 81 (1977): 306.

two aisles. Late Roman in date, it has parallels with synagogues in Galilee.[26]

## Temples

The oldest temple at Miletus was that of Athena (figure 9, #12). Archaeologists have uncovered the outline of the 7th-century B.C. structure, which was shaped as a megaron with a single row of columns. After this temple was destroyed by the Persians, a new temple in the classical Greek style was erected.

One of the later temples was dedicated to Serapis and located to the west of the South Agora. It dates from the 3rd century A.D., as indicated by an inscription of Aurelian.[27]

The most important sanctuary was the Delphinion (#3) near the southeast corner of the Lion Harbor, sacred to Apollo Delphinios, that is, the Apollo associated with the *delphis* (dolphin), a creature that served as the protector and guide of seamen. The original temenos was built in the archaic period. By the Hellenistic era it enclosed an area 50 by 60 meters (165 by 200 feet). In addition to the central altar, there were at least four portable altars. Two semicircular exedrae served for the display of statues, and a round structure probably functioned as a *heroon* or shrine for the deified founders of the city.[28]

## The Sacred Way from Miletus

Leading south of the Delphinion is the Sacred Way, which extended 12 miles to the oracular sanctuary of Apollo at Didyma (figure 8).

In the city itself the beginning of the Sacred Way was 100 meters (328 feet) long and 28 meters (92 feet) wide with pavements nearly 6 meters (20 feet) broad. To the

---

26. Kleiner, *Die Ruinen*, p. 48.
27. Ibid., p. 33; R. Salditt-Trappman, *Tempel der ägyptischen Götter in Griechenland und an der Westküste Kleinasiens* (Leiden: E. J. Brill, 1970), ch. 3.
28. Akurgal, *Ancient Civilizations*, pp. 210–11.

east of the Sacred Way (figure 9, #7) was an Ionic stoa donated by Capito, a friend of Claudius. Its seven steps were used by spectators to view the spring processional. Excavators have been working recently in this area.[29]

29. Ibid., p. 215; M. J. Mellink, "Archaeology in Asia Minor," *AJA* 76 (1972): 182; idem, *AJA* 82 (1978): 326; W. Real, V. Rödel, and M. Ueblacker, "Milet 1972," *IM* 23–24 (1973–74): 117, 125–28.

# 9

## DIDYMA

### The Sacred Way to Didyma

The emperor Trajan undertook to repave the Sacred Way from Miletus to Didyma, a distance of over 10 miles. An inscription of Trajan asserts that "turning his attention to the road necessary for the sacred rites of Apollo [of Didyma], he cut down the hills and filled in the valleys and undertook, completed and dedicated the road through Quintus Iulius Balbus, the proconsul. . . ."[1]

The Sacred Way just before it reached Didyma was lined with statues of the Branchidae, the priests and priestesses in charge of the sanctuary. (The site is sometimes called Branchidae.) Some of these seated statues were taken by C. T. Newton to the British Museum in 1858.[2] Sections of the road near the modern village of Yeni Hisar, where the ruins are now located, were uncovered in 1972. Under Klaus Tuchelt nearly 100 meters (328 feet) of the road,

---

1. Cited in G. M. A. Hanfmann, *From Croesus to Constantine* (Ann Arbor: University of Michigan Press, 1975), pp. 47–48.
2. R. Naumann, *Didyma Führer* (Istanbul: Türkiye Turing ve Otomobil Kurum, n.d.), p. 9.

which is 5 to 7 meters (16 to 23 feet) wide, have now been cleared. The earliest pavement dates to the 7th–6th centuries B.C.; level IV may be the Trajanic pavement.[3]

## Historical Background

The oracle of Apollo at Didyma played a role in the East comparable to the role of Delphi in the West. It was already established by the 8th century B.C. Herodotus records that offerings were sent to the oracle both by Necho, the Egyptian pharaoh (II.159), and by Croesus (I.92).

The archaic temple, which was built in the 6th century B.C., was destroyed by the Persians in 494 B.C. when they suppressed the Ionian Revolt. The 1962 season was the first to uncover evidence of this destruction.[4] The Persians banished the Branchidae to the eastern part of their empire, and carried off the bronze statue of Apollo to Ecbatana.

After Alexander liberated Ionia, Miletus began to rebuild the sanctuary at Didyma. The grateful oracle foretold Alexander's victory at Issus.[5] A life-size head of Alexander was recently recovered at Didyma.[6] Seleucus I Nicator recovered the cult statue in about 300 B.C.

One of the architects who worked on the Artemision at Ephesus designed the Hellenistic temple of Didyma. Whereas almost nothing remains of the Artemision, the remains of the temple at Didyma are well preserved and convey a striking impression of what the Artemision itself may have looked like.

In the Roman era Caligula sought to complete the temple. Trajan and Hadrian were both made honorary chief priests of the shrine. Finally, Julian the Apostate also contributed to the building, which was still unfinished in his day.

---

3. M. J. Mellink, "Archaeology in Asia Minor," *AJA* 80 (1976): 278–79; idem, *AJA* 82 (1978): 325.

4. R. Naumann, "Didyma," *AS* 13 (1963): 24.

5. Robert Flacelière, *Greek Oracles* (New York: W. W. Norton, 1965), pp. 30–31; W. Günther, *Das Orakel von Didyma in hellenistischer Zeit* (Tübingen: E. Wasmuth, 1971).

6. Mellink, "Archaeology in Asia Minor," *AJA* 80 (1976): 279.

Though the oracle was sacked by the Goths in 262, it continued to function. It advised Diocletian to continue his persecution against the Christians. But by the 4th century paganism was losing its battle with Christianity. Julian had to remove Christian chapels which had been placed inside the sanctuary. In the 5th century a Christian basilica was erected at the site. Destructions by fire and earthquakes forced the abandonment of Didyma by the 15th century.

## Excavations

Travelers to the area in the 18th and 19th centuries brought descriptions of the site back to Europe. Some excavations were conducted by the Frenchmen O. Rayet and A. Thomas in 1872–73 and by B. Hausoullier and E. Pontremoli in 1895–96. The Germans began their long involvement at Didyma with work from 1905 to 1913 under T. Wiegand, G. Kawerau, and H. Knackfuss. Wiegand of the Royal Prussian Museum went back to the site after World War I, and continued until his death in 1937. Since 1962 the Deutsche Archäologische Institut at Istanbul has renewed activity at Didyma under Klaus Tuchelt.

**IX.1**
The great temple of Apollo was unroofed. These are the interior stairs which led to the *naiskos* or shrine.

## The Archaic Sanctuary

According to Pausanias the temple was first established when the Ionians migrated to western Asia Minor from Greece. The earliest temenos was constructed in the late 8th century B.C., and enclosed the sacred well, the circular altar, and no doubt the laurel tree of Apollo.

The archaic Didymaion or temple building, erected in about 550 B.C., enclosed the *naiskos* or shrine (see photo IX.1). The shrine was roofed but the Didymaion was not. The Didymaion was a colossal structure 85 by 38 meters (280 by 125 feet), with 112 columns. This was the temple which was destroyed by the Persians in 494.[7]

## The Hellenistic Sanctuary

The new Hellenistic sanctuary, which was designed by Paionios, was the third largest building in the Hellenistic world after the Artemision at Ephesus and Hera's temple at Samos. Like its predecessor the unroofed Hellenistic Didymaion surrounded a small roofed *naiskos*.[8] Between the porch and the open cella was the *chrēsmographeion* or oracle room, flanked by two ramps (see photo IX.2).

The later Didymaion was somewhat larger than the earlier, 109 by 51 meters (358 by 167 feet), with 122 Ionic columns. Two of the 19.7-meter-high (65-foot) columns supporting a section of the architrave are still standing on the north side, and a third column stands on the south side (see photo IX.3). Another column lies on its side with its drums like toppled dominoes.

Ancient sources relate that the interior of the Didymaion was decorated with sculptures and paintings. On display at the site are a sculptured Medusa head from the frieze and a marvelously sculptured marble lion. Some of the columns have sculptured bases as at the Artemision

---

7. E. Akurgal, *Ancient Civilizations and Ruins of Turkey,* 2nd ed. (Istanbul: Mobil Oil Türk A.S., 1970), pp. 224–25.

8. Late Roman coins of Gordian I depict the *naiskos.* See M. J. Price and B. L. Trell, *Coins and Their Cities* (Detroit: Wayne State University Press, 1977), pp. 134–35; W. Voigtländer, "Quellhaus und Naiskos im Didymaion nach den Perserkriegen," *IM* 22 (1972): 93–107.

**IX.2**
One of the two ramps which led to the
*chresmographeion,* where the oracle of
Apollo gave answers to inquirers.

**IX.3**
Two of the original 122 Ionic
columns, standing 65 feet high,
support a section of the architrave.

**IX.4**
A sculptured column base. Similar column bases decorated the temple of Artemis at Ephesus. In fact, one of the architects who worked on the Artemision
planned the temple at Didyma.

(see photo IX.4). Not all critics find these elaborate decorations pleasing. Henri Metzger, for example, remarks:

> The profusion of ornament—columns with sculptured plinths and capitals in which heads of various deities sometimes take the place of volutes—often makes us long for the sobriety of earlier styles.[9]

## The Stadium

In the 3rd century B.C. athletic games in honor of Apollo like the Pythian games at Delphi were instituted. South of the temple was a stadium with seven rows of seats. Texts dated from 17/16 B.C. have been published which honor the *Boegos*, the priest who provided the ox to be sacrificed for Apollo and Zeus at such athletic festivals.[10]

---

9.  Henri Metzger, *Anatolia II* (London: Cresset, 1969), p. 186.

10. J. Fontenrose, "The Festival Called Boegia at Didyma," *University of* ...m, "Zeus *iation* 63

# 10

## LAODICEA

### Location

Laodicea was located in the fertile valley of the Lycus River, a tributary of the Meander River which flowed into the coast at Miletus (figure 2). It was located in the southwest part of the territory of Phrygia astride the great southern road which penetrated the interior. Roads from the western gate led to Ephesus, from the northern gate to Hierapolis, and from the eastern gate to Syria (figure 11).

Laodicea was situated on a plateau south of the Lycus River. Today the village of Eski Hissar ("Old Fortress") is found near the ruins, which are close to the modern city of Denizli 5 miles away.

### New Testament References

Laodicea (Col. 2:1; 4:13, 15, 16) is associated with Colossae, which was 10 miles east, and with Hierapolis (Col. 4:13), which was 6 miles north.[1] Laodicea may be the best known of the seven churches of Revelation (Rev. 1:11; 3:14).

1. See S. E. Johnson, "Laodicea and Its Neighbors," *BA* 13 (1950): 1–18. I have profited greatly from a paper prepared for a graduate seminar by John M. Lawrence.

**Figure 10**      **ENVIRONS OF DENIZLI**

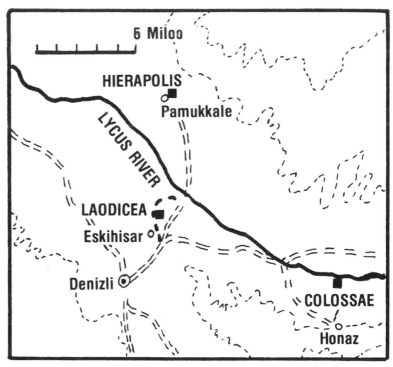

After George E. Bean, *Turkey Beyond the Meander* (London: Ernest Benn, 1971)

## Historical Background

The Laodicea in Phrygia was called "Laodicea ad Lycum" to distinguish it from eight other cities called Laodicea. It was first known as Diospolis, then as Rhoas. It was rebuilt by Antiochus II between 261 and 253 B.C., and renamed after his wife Laodice.[2] The city first appears in historical texts in 220 B.C.; some thirty years later it fell under Pergamene rule after the Peace of Apamea in 188.

Among the speeches of Cicero there is a defense of the governor Flaccus, who had seized twenty pounds of gold from the Jews at Laodicea which were to be sent to Jerusalem (*Pro Flacco* 68). W. M. Ramsay estimated that this amount of gold would be equal to fifteen thousand silver drachmae, which would represent the offering of 7,500 adult Jewish freemen.[3]

About eight years after his defense of Flaccus, Cicero was sent out as a reluctant proconsul of Cilicia. From his letters we learn that he arranged to meet his predecessor, Appius Clodius Pulcher, at Laodicea. We also learn that he intended to cash bills of exchange there, as it was a banking center, and that he later spent two-and-a-half months at Laodicea hearing cases. In a letter written to Atticus (*Ad Atticum* V.15) from Laodicea on August 3, 51 B.C., Cicero gives vent to his feelings:

> I got to Laodicea on July 31. Notch up the days of my year of office from that date. I received as warm and enthusiastic a welcome as could be; but it's incredible how bored I am with the whole business, what inadequate scope I have for my well-known mental drive and how unproductive my famous energy has become. Good God! Am I to sit in the courthouse at Laodicea, while Aulus Plotius sits at Rome?

---

2. R. C. Trench, *Commentary on the Epistles to the Seven Churches in Asia* (Minneapolis: Klock and Klock, 1978 reprint of 1897 edition), p. 200; John A. Cramer, *A Geographical and Historical Description of Asia Minor* (Amsterdam: A. M. Hakkert, 1971 reprint of the 1832 edition), vol. II, p. 38. The most thorough treatment of the city's history remains that by W. M. Ramsay in *The Cities and Bishoprics of Phrygia* (Oxford: Clarendon Press, 1895), vol. I, pp. 32–83.

3. W. M. Ramsay, *Letters to the Seven Churches* (Grand Rapids: Baker, 1979 reprint), p. 420.

## Figure 11

## PLAN OF LAODICEA

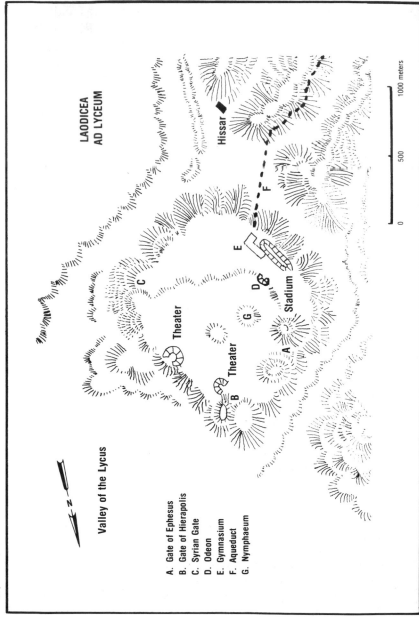

Valley of the Lycus

LAODICEA
AD LYCEUM

A. Gate of Ephesus
B. Gate of Hierapolis
C. Syrian Gate
D. Odeon
E. Gymnasium
F. Aqueduct
G. Nymphaeum

Theater

Theater

Stadium

Hissar

1000 meters

500

0

**X.1**
The as-yet-unexcavated stadium was dedicated under the emperor Titus (A.D. 79–81).

**X.2**
The gymnasium/bath was dedicated in A.D. 123/124 to the emperor Hadrian and his wife Sabina.

And when our friend Caesar has that huge army, am I to have merely a couple of skeleton legions to my credit? In any case, those are not the things I want. The big world, the public stage, the Metropolis, my home, all of you—that is what I want.[4]

Fragments of an inscription at Miletus mention the famous orator.[5]

Laodicea prospered under the Roman emperors. After the great earthquake of A.D. 17, Tiberius sent aid. But after another quake, which occurred in 60, during the

---

4. L. P. Wilkinson, *Letters of Cicero* (New York: W. W. Norton, 1968), pp. 79–80.

5. R. K. Sherk, *Roman Documents from the Greek East* (Baltimore: Johns Hopkins University Press, 1969), #52, pp. 272–76.

reign of Nero,[6] the city was wealthy enough to rebuild without further aid from the Romans (Tacitus, *Annals* XIV.27; cf. Rev. 3:17).

The city prospered especially under the Flavian emperors. The triple Syrian Gate (figure 11, C) was dedicated by Vespasian. A Greek inscription, dated 79, found on the moldings of the stadium reads:

> To the Emperor Titus Caesar Augustus Vespasian(us), Seven Times Consul, Son of the Deified Emperor Vespasian; and to the People. Nicostratus the Younger . . . dedicated . . . at his own expense; Nicostratus . . . his heir having completed what remained of the work, and Marcus Ulpius Trajanus the Proconsul having consecrated it.[7]

Marcus Ulpius Trajanus was the emperor Trajan's father and was the proconsul of Asia under Titus and Domitian. Both Nicostratus and his cousin also set up votive statues to Titus in the same year in connection with the dedication of the stadium (see figure 11, and photo X.1).

On the southeast side of the city limestone blocks from a triple-arched gateway were visible in former years. They bore Greek and Latin inscriptions to Domitian, whose name had been hacked away.

The gymnasium/bath (figure 11, E, and photo X.2) was dedicated probably in 123/124 to the emperor Hadrian and his wife Sabina. Votive dedications commemorate the emperor's visit to the city in 129.

Coins from the reign of Caracalla depict the forum with a temple which was probably of the imperial cult. The emperor is shown bestowing honors on the leading citizens of the city.[8] On another coin, Caracalla is shown sacrificing in front of a hexastyle temple with windows in the pediment.[9]

---

6. Michael Grant, *Nero* (New York: American Heritage, 1970), p. 31, reproduces a coin portrait of the young Nero from the Laodicean mint.

7. C. C. Vermeule, *Roman Imperial Art in Greece and Asia Minor* (Cambridge: Harvard University Press, 1968), pp. 238–39.

8. M. J. Price and B. L. Trell, *Coins and Their Cities* (Detroit: Wayne State University Press, 1977), pp. 25, 31.

9. Ibid., p. 129.

## The Water Supply

As there were no springs at Laodicea and as the waters of the Lycus were not dependable, the Laodiceans utilized aqueducts. Sections of an aqueduct which came from the south in the direction of Denizli (figure 11, F) are still visible. It is not correct, as some writers seem to believe, that the waters for this aqueduct came from the warm springs of Hierapolis, for that city was to the north (figure 10).

Nonetheless, it is true that the waters for the aqueducts were drawn from hot springs, as the calcareous deposits which have almost completely blocked sections of the aqueduct attest.[10] By the time the waters reached Laodicea they would have been tepid (cf. Rev. 3:16). As M. J. S. Rudwick and E. M. B. Green point out, such water would be neither therapeutically hot nor refreshingly cold.[11] E. M. Blaiklock comments:

> In the gardens of Te Aroha, or at a spring near Lake Rotoma in New Zealand, such warm soda-laden waters may be tasted with the immediate temptation to do as the writer to Laodicea threatens he will do. The sickly mixture, neither refreshingly cold, not beneficently hot, and burdened with alien content, disgusts.[12]

## The Nymphaeum

From 1961 to 1963 Laval University in Quebec under Jean des Gagniers completely cleared an elaborate nymphaeum or fountain house (figure 11, G), which was built not earlier than the 3rd century A.D. The nymphaeum included a square water basin, two semicircular fountains, and storage chambers. A colossal statue of Isis or of one of

---

10. C. J. Hemer, "Unto the Angels of the Churches," *BH* 11 (1975): 177. Note the cover photo.

11. M. J. S. Rudwick and E. M. B. Green, "The Laodicean Lukewarmness," *Expository Times* 69 (1957–58): 176–78; Hemer, "Unto the Angels," pp. 181–83.

12. E. M. Blaiklock, *The Cities of the New Testament* (London: Pickering & Inglis, 1965), p. 125.

her priestesses was found at the site. Carved crosses indicate that in its later stages the building was used by Christians.[13]

## The Stadium and the Games

Gladiatorial games were being held at Laodicea as early as 50 B.C., as a letter of Cicero (*Ad Atticum* VI.3.9) attests: "Another thing I may as well mention is that Hortensius junior was in Laodicea for the gladiators [*Laodiceae gladiatoribus*]."[14]

The stadium (figure 11), 1000 feet in length, was an enclosed structure for gladiatorial games. As noted above (p. 140), it was dedicated to Vespasian and Titus by a wealthy family. The city set up an inscription recognizing the benefactions of the family, which reads as follows:

> The council and the people have honored Tatia, daughter of Nicostratos, son of Pericles, who died young, for the sake of the magistracies, services, and supervision of public works filled by her father and for the cause of his grand uncle Nicostratos who, in other services, has been priest of the city, and has consecrated the amphitheater stadium in white marble.[15]

Funerary inscriptions refer to those who fought and died in the games. Ramsay discussed one inscription which marked "the tombs of the gladiators at the show given by Diokles, high-priest and stephanēphoros."[16]

---

13. In addition to the final report of Jean des Gagniers et al., *Laodicée du Lycos: Le Nymphée, Campagnes, 1961–1963* (Quebec: l'Université Laval, 1969), see also Otto F. A. Meinardus, *St. John of Patmos and the Seven Churches of the Apocalypse* (Athens: Lycabettus, 1974), pp. 132–33; and *Bible et Terre Sainte* 81 (March, 1966), which contains articles on Laodicea by M. Bobichon, P. Devambez, R. Leconte, and J. Maigret.

14. *Cicero's Letters to Atticus*, ed. D. R. Schackleton Bailey (Cambridge: Cambridge University Press, 1968), vol. III, pp. 120–21; David Magie, *Roman Rule in Asia Minor* (Princeton: Princeton University Press, 1950), vol. I, p. 127; vol. II, pp. 986–87.

15. Louis Robert in Gagniers, *Laodicée*, p. 323.

16. Ramsay, *The Cities and Bishoprics*, vol. I, pp. 75–77; Louis Robert, *Les Gladiateurs dans l'Orient Grec* (Amsterdam: A. M. Hakkert, 1971 reprint of 1941 edition), pp. 151–52.

To the east of the stadium is the large building (figure 11, E) which, as we have already noted, has been interpreted as a gymnasium/bath dedicated to Hadrian. This is indicated by an inscription on the occasion of his visit in 129, or possibly of an earlier visit in 123.[17]

An inscription as interpreted by Louis Robert indicates that there were also musical contests held in Laodicea. The text describes the fifty-seven victories of a solo *aulētēs*, that is, one who played the *aulos,* an instrument which is most often translated "flute" but which was closer to an oboe.[18] One of the thirty-three contests where he won these victories was held at Laodicea.[19]

## The Theaters

As yet unexcavated are the large theater (see photo X.3), which is Greek in date, the small Roman theater (see photo X.4), and the *odeion* (figure 11, D).[20] A block dedicated to Hadrian and to Aelius Caesar, dated to 136/137, was found in the large theater.[21]

## Gods and Goddesses

Coins and inscriptions reveal the names of many gods and goddesses worshiped at Laodicea. The most important deity was Zeus Laodicenus. His temple was probably the largest in the city, but we are ignorant of its location. We know that a white pavement was laid in front of it.[22]

Other gods honored were Dionysus, Helios, Nemesis, Hades/Serapis, and Mithras. Among the goddesses that were venerated were Hera, Athena, Tyche, and the Syrian

---

17. Ramsay, *The Cities and Bishoprics,* vol. I, pp. 47–48.

18. Warren D. Anderson, *Ethos and Education in Greek Music* (Cambridge: Harvard University Press, 1966), p. 8: "The term 'flute' is inadmissible: the aulos had a reed mouthpiece like that found on an oboe, not the right-angled aperture of a modern concert flute."

19. Robert in Gagniers, *Laodicée,* p. 293.

20. E. Akurgal, *Ancient Civilizations and Ruins of Turkey,* 2nd ed. (Istanbul: Mobil Oil Türk A.S., 1970), p. 237.

21. Vermeule, *Roman Imperial Art,* p. 474.

22. Robert in Gagniers, *Laodicée,* p. 275.

**X.3** The large theater is Greek in date.

**X.4** The small theater is Roman in date.

Aphrodite.[23] The eponymous founder of the city, Laodice, was also worshiped.[24]

## Divination and Healing

The Laodiceans paid particular reverence to Apollo, the god of prophecy, and to Asklepios, the god of healing. A series of inscriptions at the shrine of Apollo at Claros, northwest of Ephesus, attests the regular consultation of the oracle by the city of Laodicea. Robert has collected twenty-five inscriptions from Claros which list "prophets" of Apollo from Laodicea.[25]

Ramsay was inclined to view Apollo, Asklepios, and even Zeus Laodicenus as simply the Hellenistic manifestations of the local god Men Karou.[26] Robert objects to such a merging of what were distinct deities. There is not, in his view, the least indication of an assimilation, or even of a rapprochement, between Asklepios and Men. Each of these gods appears on the coins with his own attributes.[27] (See p. 68.)

A dozen miles northwest of Laodicea was the temple of Men Karou, which was famed as a medical school (Strabo XII.8.20). Circumstantial evidence indicates that there may have been a medical school at Laodicea itself which specialized in dispensing collyrium, used as an eyesalve and as a cosmetic.[28] According to the famous Pergamene physician, Galen:

---

23. Ibid., p. 257.

24. Ibid., pp. 324–25. Robert interprets an inscription (MAMA VI, 18) as belonging to her cult rather than as an inscription of a priest for Zeus as Ramsay had held.

25. Robert in Gagniers, *Laodicée*, pp. 298–303. On Claros, see Robert Flacelière, *Greek Oracles* (New York: W. W. Norton, 1965), pp. 44–47.

26. Ramsay, *The Cities and Bishoprics*, vol. I, pp. 52–53.

27. Robert in Gagniers, *Laodicée*, pp. 290–91.

28. Hemer, "Unto the Angels," p. 189, n. 34, writes: "The statement that an eyesalve was made at Laodicea, often taken from Ramsay, *Seven Churches*, pp. 419, 429, is not an attested fact, but is based on his inference.... There is however circumstantial support for the inference, and there are independent grounds for locating an advanced and specialised ophthalmology at Laodicea."

And the eyes you will strengthen by using the dry collyrium made of Phrygian stone, applying the mixture to the eyelids without touching the membrane of the eye inside. For this is what women do every day, when they make their eyes glamorous. (*de Sanitate Tuenda* XII)[29]

Commentators have seen in Revelation 3:18 an allusion to the "eyesalve" of the region.[30] C. J. Hemer concludes:

The church is judged as "poor and blind and naked," but Laodicea boasted businesses and manufactures which professed to meet each of these needs: it was a banking centre famous for its eye-surgeons and ointments and for its woollen clothing. The church no doubt regarded itself as spiritually rich and perhaps intellectually superior. It was blind to its own blindness.[31]

---

29. Galen, *De Sanitate Tuenda*, tr. R. M. Green (Springfield, IL: Charles C. Thomas, 1951), p. 269.
30. Robert H. Mounce, *The Book of Revelation* (Grand Rapids: Wm. B. Eerdmans, 1977), p. 127.
31. Hemer, "Unto the Angels," p. 183.

# 11

## HIERAPOLIS

### Location

*Hierapolis* ("The Holy City") was known as *Hieropolis* ("City of the Sanctuary") until about the time of Augustus. Hierapolis was located 6 miles north of Laodicea on a plateau 300 feet above the plain. Its gleaming white calcareous terraces, like those of Mammoth Springs in Yellowstone, deposited by its warm springs are clearly visible from Laodicea, and have given it the picturesque Turkish name of *Pamukkale* ("Cotton Castle") (see photo XI.1). The site is now a popular tourist resort. As Sybille Haynes notes, "To the west of the colonnaded street and a short distance below the Nymphaeum lies the Sacred Pool, which is now profanely enclosed by a motel and serves as its swimming-pool."[1]

### New Testament Reference

The only New Testament reference is Colossians 4:13. Later in the Christian Era, the tradition arose that Philip made his home here (see p. 154).

---

1. Sybille Haynes, *Land of the Chimaera* (New York: St. Martin's Press, 1974), p. 135.

**XI.1**
The white calcareous terraces which give the site its modern name, *Pamukkale* ("Cotton Castle").

The most famous figure to come from Hierapolis was the slave Epictetus, born about A.D. 50, who eventually became an outstanding Stoic philosopher. F. W. Farrar speculates:

> If Epictetus spent any part of his boyhood there, he might have conversed with men and women of humble rank who had heard read in their obscure place of meeting the Epistle of St. Paul to the Colossians, and the other, now lost, which he addressed to the Church of Laodicea.[2]

## Historical Background

There has been a long-standing controversy as to whether Hierapolis was founded by the Pergamenes or Seleucids. The earliest extant inscription from Hierapolis is that of the mother of the Pergamene king Eumenes II (197–159 B.C.). Since nearby Laodicea is known to have been found-

2. F. W. Farrar, *Seekers After God* (London: Macmillan, 1891), pp. 187–88.

ed by the Seleucids, scholars have assumed that they would not have founded another city so close by.[3] On the other hand, V. Tcherikover has argued that Hierapolis was also a Seleucid city.

The dispute has now been settled in favor of the latter view by the discovery of Seleucid tribal names in an inscription from the theater.[4] F. Kolb argues that Hierapolis was probably founded by Antiochus I before Antiochus II established Laodicea.

After being eclipsed by Laodicea for about three centuries, Hierapolis became preeminent at the end of the 1st century A.D. and flourished especially during the 2nd and 3rd centuries.

A bilingual inscription on the triple ceremonial gate in the northern part of the city, dated between A.D. 84 and 86, once contained Domitian's name, which has suffered damage. A cuirassed statue, perhaps of Hadrian, has been recovered from the temple of Apollo.[5] The most splendid monuments, such as the theater, were erected under Septimius Severus and Caracalla.

### Excavations

Full-scale excavations have been conducted since 1957 under the Italian archaeologist, Paolo Verzone. He has concentrated on excavating and restoring the temple of Apollo, the theater, the nymphaeum, and the baths.

As nothing remains of the Hellenistic city, the visible monuments are of the Roman period. The main colonnaded street runs over a mile in a north-south direction. Extensive sections of the city walls survive except on the west. Channels for distributing the water from the hot springs are visible throughout the site (see photo XI.2). Sewer channels ran down the center of each street.

3. George E. Bean, *Turkey Beyond the Maeander* (London: Ernest Benn, 1971), p. 234.

4. F. Kolb, "Zur Geschichte der Stadt Hierapolis in Phrygien: Die Phyleninschriften im Theater," *Zeitschrift für Papyrologie und Epigraphik* 15 (1974): 255-70.

5. C. C. Vermeule, *Roman Imperial Art in Greece and Asia Minor* (Cambridge: Harvard University Press, 1968), pp. 472–73.

**XI.2** A channel for distributing water from the hot springs.

## The Temple of Apollo

Though an earlier sanctuary may have gone back to the Hellenistic age, the temple of Apollo under present consideration dates no earlier than the 3rd century A.D.[6] It rests on the site of an oracle of Apollo which was consulted on the occasion of a plague under Marcus Aurelius.

---

6. For a numismatic representation see M. J. Price and B. L. Trell, *Coins and Their Cities* (Detroit: Wayne State University Press, 1977), p. 197. Though the structure of only one temple has so far been identified at Hierapolis, coins indicate that there were other temples dedicated to Dionysus, to the emperor Caracalla, etc. See Price and Trell, *Coins and Their Cities*, pp. 197, 264.

The oracle recommended sacrifices especially to the Apollo of Claros, "For you are sprung from me and from Mopsos, the protector of your city."[7] Mopsos, the legendary seer of Claros, led a contingent of Greeks after the Trojan War to a settlement in Cilicia in southwestern Anatolia.[8] The discovery of a bilingual Phoenician and Hittite hieroglyphic text at Karatepe lends substance to the tradition.[9]

## The Plutonium

Hierapolis was famed as the location of the Plutonium, the reputed entrance to the underworld. According to Strabo (XIII.4.14), only the eunuch priests of Pluto were able to descend unharmed into the hole, the poisonous fumes of which instantly killed the bulls which they took down with them.

By the 4th century A.D. the hole had been blocked up so that eventually its location was forgotten. W. M. Ramsay comments, "I think we must attribute it to the action of the Christians, who had deliberately filled up and covered over the place, the very dwelling-place of Satan."[10]

The Italian excavators have now rediscovered the Plutonium on the south side of the temple of Apollo. They have uncovered a chamber 9 feet square from which the sound of fast-flowing water may be heard, and from which odoriferous vapor may be smelled.[11]

W. C. Brice, who descended into another cavity at Hierapolis in 1950, has been able to explain the ancient phenomena described by Strabo:

The air felt warm and heavy to about knee height, and a burning match lowered to this level was immediately extin-

---

7. Bean, *Turkey*, p. 241; G. P. Carratelli, "ΧΡΗΣΜΟΙ di Apollo Kareios e Apollo Klarios a Hierapolis in Frigia," *Annuario della Scuola Archeologia di Atene* 25–26 (1963–64): 352–70.

8. R. D. Barnett, "Mopsus," *Journal of Hellenic Studies* 73 (1953): 140–43.

9. H. T. Bossert, "Die Phönizisch-Hethitischen Bilinguen vom Karatepe," *Oriens* 2 (1949): 72–128.

10. W. M. Ramsay, *The Cities and Bishoprics of Phrygia* (Oxford: Clarendon Press, 1895), vol. I, p. 86.

11. Bean, *Turkey*, p. 237.

guished. I lowered my head cautiously, and discovered that it was quite impossible to breathe inside this accumulation of gas.... The gas concerned was undoubtedly carbon dioxide, which can be seen bubbling through the swimming pools of warm water on the surface of the plateau.... Being heavier than air, the carbon dioxide would stay low, so that a bull's head would be within the gas, while its custodian could breathe above the danger level.[12]

## Textiles

The thermal waters of the city aided its "purple" textile industry. According to David Magie, "It was said that the water of the city, heavily charged with lime, was so well suited for dyeing that the purple wool, which was dyed with madder-root, rivalled that which was elsewhere treated with cochineal or the genuine purple mussel."[13]

Inscriptions dated from the 2nd and 3rd centuries A.D. list *porphyrabaphoi* ("purple dyers"), carpet weavers, and wool washers. There is evidence that Jews were members of the first two guilds, and that they may even have dominated the first.[14]

## The Theater

The Italians have spent much effort since 1958 clearing and restoring the well-preserved theater. The large structure has a frontage of about 100 meters (over 325 feet). The cavea has fifty rows of seats, with a royal box in the center.

The 12-foot-high stage is decorated with reliefs depicting episodes from the lives of Dionysus, Artemis, and Apollo. One relief portrays Chrysoroas, who was the personification of the fumes of Hierapolis. Other reliefs show a sacrificial scene on which are portrayed the imperial fig-

---

12. W. C. Brice, "A Note on the Descent into the Plutonium at Hierapolis of Phrygia," *Journal of Semitic Studies* 23 (1978): 226–27.
13. David Magie, *Roman Rule in Asia Minor* (Princeton: Princeton University Press, 1950), vol. I, p. 48.
14. W. M. Ramsay, *The Social Basis of Roman Power in Asia Minor* (Amsterdam: A. M. Hakkert, 1967), p. 170; S. Safrai and M. Stern, eds., *The Jewish People in the First Century* (Philadelphia: Fortress Press, 1974), p. 480; Haynes, *Land of the Chimaera*, p. 137.

ures of Septimius Severus, Caracalla, and Geta, and must therefore be dated to between 204 and 211.[15]

## Gladiatorial Games

As there is no sign of a stadium on the plateau, athletic contests may have been held on the plain. Gladiatorial and wild-beast shows were evidently given in the theater.[16] According to Louis Robert, the necropolis of Hierapolis provides an outstanding ensemble of inscriptions of fallen gladiators.[17] One epitaph commemorates a gladiator who was crowned ten times.[18]

## The Necropolis

The cemetery, which extends 2 kilometers (1¼ mile) north of the city, dates from the late Hellenistic period to the early Christian Era. It contains twelve hundred tombs, three hundred of them with epitaphs. George E. Bean cites as a typical curse upon tomb violators the following inscription:

> May he who commits transgression, and he who incites thereto, have no joy of life or children, may he find no land to tread nor sea to sail, but childless and destitute, crippled by every form of affliction let him perish, and after death may he meet the wrath and vengeance of the gods below. And the same curses [fall] on those who fail to prosecute him.[19]

The tombs provide us with some of our best information not only on the gladiators, but also on the Jews of the community. To illustrate the position of Saul of Tarsus,

---

15. Bean, *Turkey*, p. 242; Daria de Bernardi Ferrero, *Teatri Classici in Asia Minore* I (Rome: "L'Erma" di Bretschneider, 1966), pp. 57–76; P. Verzone, "Le campagne a Hierapolis di Frigia," *Annuario della Scuola Archeologia di Atene* 23–24 (1961–62): 633–47; 25–26 (1963–64): 352–70.

16. Bean, *Turkey*, p. 238.

17. Louis Robert, *Études Anatoliennes* (Amsterdam: A. M. Hakkert, 1970 reprint of 1937 edition), p. 308.

18. Louis Robert, *Les Gladiateurs dans l'Orient Grec* (Amsterdam: A. M. Hakkert, 1971 reprint of 1941 edition), p. 155, #124.

19. Bean, *Turkey*, p. 245.

who was both a citizen of his city and a Roman citizen, F. F. Bruce cites an epitaph from Hierapolis which refers to a "Marcus Aurelius Alexander, also called Asaph, of the people of the Jews."[20]

## The Martyrium of Philip

One of the most interesting structures at Hierapolis is the octagonal Martyrium of Philip located outside the city walls on the northeast slopes of the hill. An octagonal chamber set within a 20-meter (66-foot) square contained a semicircular bench for the clergy and a lectern.[21] Eight small chapels for pilgrims radiated from the central chamber. The Martyrium, which was built in the 5th century, was cleared by the excavators in 1957–58.[22]

There are two possible candidates for the Philip who was commemorated here: either Philip the Apostle or Philip the Deacon Evangelist. Polycrates, the bishop of Ephesus (c. 190), identified the subject as Philip the Apostle, a view which was favored by Ramsay.[23] On the other hand, the Montanists, who claimed that the Holy Spirit inspired their prophetesses, cited the example of the four daughters of Philip the Deacon, whose tombs were still to be seen at Hierapolis (see Eusebius, *Historia Ecclesiastica* III.31.4). Bruce favors the view that the Martyrium commemorates this Philip (Acts 21:8–9).[24]

---

20. F. F. Bruce, *Paul: Apostle of the Heart Set Free* (Grand Rapids: Wm. B. Eerdmans, 1977), p. 36, n. 11.

21. Haynes, *Land of the Chimaera*, p. 134.

22. P. Verzone, "Il martyrium ottagono a Hierapolis di Frigia," *Palladio* 10 (1960): 1–20.

23. W. M. Ramsay, "Hierapolis," *Dictionary of the Bible*, ed. James Hastings (New York: Scribner, 1899), vol. II, p. 380; so also E. Akurgal, *Ancient Civilizations and Ruins of Turkey*, 2nd ed. (Istanbul: Mobil Oil Türk A.S., 1970), p. 175; and Haynes, *Land of the Chimaera*, p. 134.

24. Bruce, *Paul*, pp. 343, 376; so also D. Boyd, "Hierapolis," *IDBS*, p. 411.

# 12

## COLOSSAE

### Location

The site of Colossae was located near Laodicea and Hierapolis in the Lycus River valley (see figure 10). The *hüyük* (Turkish for "tell" or mound) covering the remains of the ancient city was identified by William J. Hamilton in 1835. By the 8th century A.D. citizens were moving away from Colossae for the safer city of Khonai (modern Honaz) 3 miles to the south on the north slopes of Mount Cadmus (see photos XII.1–3).

Herodotus (VII.30) claimed that Colossae was located near a river which ran underground for 5 stades (about two-thirds of a mile). Though his statement was not literally accurate, the Lycus River does run in a narrow gorge (see photo XII.4).

As the Greek name of the city *(Kolossai)* was similar to the word for the colossal statue on Rhodes *(kolossos),* which was one of the Seven Wonders of the World, a tradition arose in the Middle Ages which held that Paul's Epistle to the Colossians was sent to the Rhodians.[1]

---

1. Otto F. A. Meinardus, "Colossus, Colossae, Colossi: Confusio Colossaea," *BA* 36 (1973): 33–36.

**XII.1**
Looking north at Colossae Hüyük (the Turkish word for a ''tell'' or mound).
*(Courtesy of Harold Mare)*

**XII.2**
Looking southwest at Colossae Hüyük.
*(Courtesy of Harold Mare)*

**XII.3**
Fragments of building materials protrude from the surface of the mound of
Colossae Hüyük. *(Courtesy of Harold Mare)*

## New Testament References

Evidently Paul had not personally evangelized Colossae
(Col. 1:4; 2:1), but during his long stay in Ephesus (Acts
19:10) he probably converted the Colossian Epaphras
(Col. 1:7; 4:12–13). Later while in prison in Rome, Paul
converted the runaway slave Onesimus, and sent him back
to his master Philemon in Colossae, bearing the letters to
the Colossians and to Philemon (Col. 4:9; Philem. 10–12).
Paul's letter to the Colossians warned the believers against
a Jewish heresy, which some have identified as a proto-
Gnostic heresy.[2]

## Historical Background

In describing the passage of Xerxes past Colossae in the
early 5th century B.C., Herodotus (VII.30) speaks of it as
"a great city." Colossae's significance lay in her strategic
position on the great southern highway which traversed
the interior of Asia Minor.

Colossae was famed for her wool, which was dyed
purple/red. (See pp. 52–54 on the dyeing industry.) Its
distinctive tint was known as *colossinus*.

Shortly after 400 B.C. Xenophon *(Anabasis* I.2.6) spoke
of Colossae as a large and prosperous city. Pliny the Elder
referred to Colossae as one of the most famous towns of
Phrygia. The establishment of Laodicea, 10 miles away, by
Antiochus II in the 3rd century B.C., led to the eventual
decline of Colossae (see p. 137).

A passage in Strabo (XII.576) has been interpreted as an
indication that Colossae was reduced to a small town at the
beginning of the Christian Era. But as W. Harold Mare
points out, there is a gap in the preserved text which ren-
ders such an interpretation problematic.[3]

2. See E. M. Yamauchi, "Qumran and Colossae," *Bibliotheca Sacra* 121
(1964): 141–52; idem, *Pre-Christian Gnosticism* (Grand Rapids: Wm. B.
Eerdmans, 1973), pp. 44–47; F. O. Francis and W. A. Meeks, eds.,
*Conflict at Colossae* (Missoula, MT: Society of Biblical Literature, 1973).
3. W. Harold Mare, "Archaeological Prospects at Colossae," *NEASB* 7
(1976): 42. What follows is largely dependent upon the observations
made by Mare and Donald Burdick in their visit in 1975, reported in

**XII.4**
The Lycus River with the ancient mound in the background. *(Courtesy of Harold Mare)*

In the Byzantine era when the area became subject to attacks from marauding Saracens and Sassanians, the inhabitants of Colossae sought refuge at Khonai. W. M. Ramsay's list of bishops reveals the gradual abandonment of Colossae in favor of Khonai during the 8th and 9th centuries.[4]

North of Colossae across the Lycus River the Church of St. Michael was erected in gratitude for the archangel's help in averting damage from the flooding of the Lycus River. The Church of Michael the Archistrategos must have been built between A.D. 450 and the 7th century. The Seljuk Turks in their first raid through the Lycus Valley in 1070 desecrated the church, using it as a stable.[5]

## Visible Remains

The mound of Colossae has never been excavated. Since 1975 the Near East Archaeological Society has been applying to the Turkish government for permission to excavate there, but no permits for new excavations are presently being granted in Turkey.

As measured by Mare and Donald Burdick the acropolis is 55 by 114 meters (180 by 370 feet). The mound rises some 50 to 75 feet above the level of the plain. Numerous building remains are visible on the acropolis, its slopes, and the plain below. Though it is now closed, George Bean reports that he was able to descend into a shaft on the western end of the mound on a long rope until he encountered difficulty breathing.[6]

The remains of the theater are located about 100 meters (330 feet) southeast of the acropolis. Mare reports:

---

this article. I was able to visit the site in 1974, traversing the very rough road from Honaz to the mound. Mare describes a much better route to get to the site (pp. 46–47).

4. W. M. Ramsay, *The Cities and Bishoprics of Phrygia* (Oxford: Clarendon Press, 1895), vol. I, p. 234.

5. Ibid., vol. I, pp. 215–16.

6. George E. Bean, *Turkey Beyond the Maeander* (London: Ernest Benn, 1971), p. 258.

The cavea where the ancient theater was situated was a semicircular hollow, 60 paces across north-south at the widest point and covered with small rocks. On the north side up the slope of the cavea a two to three course wall of cut stone was seen, no doubt part of the wall structure of the theater.[7]

The necropolis of the city was located north of the acropolis across the Lycus River. Rectangular tombs were cut close together into the porous rock ledge. Mare notes of the tombs:

These were cut rather close to one another, with narrow ledges cut around the outer edges of the graves onto which stone lids were set at ground level. . . . Though the graves visible today have been robbed, meaningful excavation work needs to be done here to analyze the meaning of the graves thus far exposed and to search for other graves in the area.[8]

When W. J. Hamilton first viewed the site in the 19th century, there were far more visible remains: He saw:

a field full of large blocks of stone and foundations of buildings, with fragments of columns and broken pottery strewed upon the ground. Others were strewed about on all sides and the road was lined with marble blocks from ancient buildings amongst which were fragments of columns, architraves, and cornices. A little farther, near the roadside, was the hollow cavea of a theatre, built on the side of a low-sloping hill, and of which several seats were still *in situ*. . . .[9]

The disappearance of these many monumental fragments underscores the urgent need for the expeditious excavation of Colossae.

### Inscriptions

Though no systematic excavations have yet been conducted, a number of inscriptions have been recovered from Colossae and its environs:

---

7.  Mare, "Colossae," p. 49.
8.  Ibid., p. 50.
9.  W. J. Hamilton, *Researches in Asia Minor, Pontus, and Armenia* (London: J. Murray, 1842), pp. 509–10, cited by Mare, "Colossae," p. 50.

(1) An inscription of a runner who was twice victorious in the stadion race was found at Honaz on an altar dedicated to Trajan.[10]

(2) Another athletic inscription and an altar dedicated to Hadrian by a tribunus militum were reported by J. C. Anderson.[11]

(3) C. C. Vermeule reports a bronze which represents the genius of the Demos (People) as a young man with a four-horse chariot of Helios; it is dated about A.D. 200.[12]

(4) From the early 4th century A.D. come a dedication to Constantius I, and another dedication possibly to Diocletian.[13]

Still other inscriptions from Colossae have been reported by Louis Robert.[14]

10. M. Clerc, "Inscriptions de la Vallée du Méandre," *Bulletin de correspondance hellénique* 11 (1887): 353–54.

11. J. C. Anderson, "A Summer in Phrygia II," *Journal of Hellenic Studies* 18 (1898): 90.

12. C. C. Vermeule, *Roman Imperial Art in Greece and Asia Minor* (Cambridge: Harvard University Press, 1968), p. 163.

13. W. H. Buckler and W. M. Calder, *Monumenta Asiae Minoris Antiqua* VI: *Monuments and Documents from Phrygia and Caria* (Manchester: Manchester University Press, 1939), pp. 15–18.

14. Louis Robert, "Les inscriptions," in Jean des Gagniers et al., *Laodicée du Lycos: Le Nymphée, Campagnes, 1961–1963* (Quebec: l'Université Laval, 1969), pp. 269, 277–78, 306, 328.

# 13

## RIVALRY AMONG CITIES

The picture which emerges from the inscriptions, the numismatic evidence, and the literary references is that of an intense and oftentimes acrimonious rivalry among the Greco-Roman cities of Asia Minor for preeminence. No longer independent, the cities had to appeal to the Roman emperor for his recognition and his gifts.

Ephesus claimed to be the "First and Greatest Metropolis of Asia" as the site of the Artemision; Pergamum boasted that it was the first official Roman capital; Smyrna claimed to be the "First of Asia in size and beauty"; and Sardis maintained that it was the "First Metropolis of Asia and all Lydia."[1]

Aristides, the famous orator, eulogized the three chief cities—Pergamum, Smyrna, and Ephesus—but begged them to restore concord among themselves.[2] C. P. Jones observes:

---

1. W. M. Ramsay, *Letters to the Seven Churches* (Grand Rapids: Baker, 1979), pp. 139–40; David Magie, *Roman Rule in Asia Minor* (Princeton: Princeton University Press, 1950), vol. I, p. 635.

2. C. J. Cadoux, *Ancient Smyrna* (Oxford: B. Blackwell, 1938), p. 275; C. P. Jones, *The Roman World of Dio Chrysostom* (Cambridge: Harvard University Press, 1978), p. 86.

The quarrel of Ephesus and Smyrna is comparatively well attested, since it became entangled in the professional rivalries of the Second Sophistic: thus, Dio's two most eminent pupils, Favorinus and Polemo, were the leading sophist of Ephesus and Smyrna respectively and bitterly hostile to each other.[3]

The dispute between Smyrna and Ephesus was to continue into the 3rd century A.D.

The historian Dio Cassius (2nd/3rd centuries A.D.) offered the following advice to the emperor:

> It is an excellent achievement also to render private disputes as few as possible and their settlement as rapid as may be. But it is best of all to cut short the impetuosity of communities and, if they appeal to your sovereignty and safety and good fortune and endeavor to force upon anybody or to undertake exploits or expenditures that are beyond their power, not to permit it. You should abolish altogether their enmities and rivalries among themselves and not authorize them to create any empty titles or anything else which will breed differences between them.[4]

The failure to address a city by its proper title was regarded as a mortal insult. We have a letter from Antoninus Pius to the Ephesians, which urges the Ephesians and the Smyrnaeans to use the correct titles in addressing each other:

> I am informed that the Pergamenes in their letter to you use the titles which I declared your city should use. But I think that the Smyrnaeans have inadvertently omitted them in the decree about the common sacrifice, but will for the future willingly conform, if you also, in your letters to them, allude to their city in the terms which are proper and have been decided.[5]

When we understand the fact that in the milieu of the early Roman Empire, one's loyalty was primarily to one's city,[6] we can understand the pride that induced Paul to

---

3. Jones, *Roman World*, p. 78.
4. *A History of Rome Through the Fifth Century* II: *The Empire*, ed. A. H. M. Jones (New York: Harper & Row, 1970), p. 68.
5. Ibid., p. 229.
6. One's loyalty was not necessarily restricted to the city of one's birth.

inform the captain of the Roman cohort that he was from Tarsus, "no mean city" (Acts 21:39). When Paul chided the Corinthians with the example of the zeal of the churches in Macedonia (Thessalonica and Philippi) for collecting funds for the poor (2 Cor. 9:1–4), he was consciously appealing to civic pride.

Not all may agree with W. M. Ramsay's practical application, but none can dispute his insight when he writes:

> It is evident that the writer of the Seven Letters did not discourage such feelings of attachment to one's native city, but encouraged local patriotism and used it as a basis on which to hold up a strenuous Christian life. The practical effect of such teaching as this is that a Christian could be a patriot, proud of and interested in the glory and history of his own city.[7]

---

Athletes and famous rhetors were claimed by adoptive cities. Dio Chrysostom's pupil Polemo noted his double devotion to his native Laodicea and his adopted Smyrna. Aristides was claimed by Pergamum, Smyrna, and Ephesus.

7. Ramsay, *Letters to the Seven Churches*, p. 277.

## THE ROMAN EMPERORS*

| | |
|---|---|
| Augustus | B.C. 27–A.D. 14 |
| Tiberius | A.D. 14–37 |
| Caligula | 37–41 |
| Claudius | 41–54 |
| Nero | 54–68 |
| Vespasian | 69–79 |
| Titus | 79–81 |
| Domitian | 81–96 |
| Nerva | 96–98 |
| Trajan | 98–117 |
| Hadrian | 117–138 |
| Antoninus Pius | 138–161 |
| Marcus Aurelius | 161–180 |
| Commodus | 180–192 |
| Septimius Severus | 193–211 |
| Caracalla | 211–217 |
| Elagabalus | 218–222 |
| Severus Alexander | 222–235 |
| Maximinus | 235–238 |
| Gordian III | 238–244 |
| Philip | 244–249 |
| Decius | 249–251 |
| Gallus | 251–253 |
| Valerianus | 253–260 |
| Gallienus | 253–268 |
| Claudius Gothicus | 268–270 |
| Aurelian | 270–275 |
| Tacitus | 275–276 |
| Probus | 276–282 |
| Numerianus | 283–284 |
| Diocletian | 284–305 |
| Constantine | 306–337 |

*Names of the more ephemeral emperors and of
rivals are omitted.

# BIBLIOGRAPHY

*Note:* Classical citations have been made from the volumes of the Loeb Classical Library.

Akurgal, Ekrem. *Ancient Civilizations and Ruins of Turkey.* 2nd ed. Istanbul: Mobil Oil Türk A.S., 1970.

Bammer, Anton. *Die Architektur des jüngeren Artemision von Ephesos.* Wiesbaden: F. Steiner, 1972.

Bean, George E. *Turkey Beyond the Maeander.* London: Ernest Benn, 1971.

Behr, C. A. *Aelius Aristides and the Sacred Tales.* Amsterdam: A. M. Hakkert, 1968.

Bernardi Ferrero, Daria de. *Teatri Classici in Asia Minore* I. Rome: "L'Erma" di Bretschneider, 1966.

_____. *Teatri Classici in Asia Minore* III. Rome: "L'Erma" di Bretschneider, 1970.

Blaiklock, E. M. *The Cities of the New Testament.* London: Pickering & Inglis, 1965.

Bowersock, G. W. *Augustus and the Greek World.* Oxford: Clarendon Press, 1965.

_____. *Greek Sophists in the Roman Empire.* Oxford: Clarendon Press, 1969.

Bruce, F. F. *Paul: Apostle of the Heart Set Free.* Grand Rapids: Wm. B. Eerdmans, 1977.

Cadoux, C. J. *Ancient Smyrna.* Oxford: B. Blackwell, 1938.

Cook, J. M. *The Greeks in Ionia and the East.* New York: F. Praeger, 1963.

Cramer, John A. *A Geographical and Historical Description of Asia Minor.* Amsterdam: A. M. Hakkert, 1971 reprint of the 1832 edition.

Deissmann, Adolf. *Light from the Ancient East.* Grand Rapids: Baker, 1965 reprint of the 1922 edition.

Dewdney, J. C. *Turkey.* New York: F. Praeger, 1971.

Gagniers, Jean des, et al. *Laodicée du Lycos: Le Nymphée, Campagnes, 1961–1963.* Quebec: l'Université Laval, 1969.

Gasque, W. W. *Sir William M. Ramsay.* Grand Rapids: Baker, 1966.

Götze, B. "Antike Bibliotheken." *Jahrbuch der Deutschen Archäologischen Instituts* 52 (1937): 225–47.

Grant, Michael. *Nero.* New York: American Heritage, 1970.

Hanfmann, G. M. A. *From Croesus to Constantine.* Ann Arbor: University of Michigan Press, 1975.

_____. *Letters from Sardis.* Cambridge: Harvard University Press, 1972.

Hansen, E. V. *The Attalids of Pergamon.* Ithaca: Cornell University Press, 1947.

Haynes, Sybille. *Land of the Chimaera.* New York: St. Martin's Press, 1974.

Hemer, C. J. "Unto the Angels of the Churches." *BH* 11 (1975): 4–27, 56–83, 110–35, 164–90.

*A History of Rome Through the Fifth Century* II: *The Empire.* Edited by A. H. M. Jones. New York: Harper & Row, 1970

Jones, C. P. *The Roman World of Dio Chrysostom.* Cambridge: Harvard University Press, 1978.

Keil, J. *Ephesos: Ein Führer durch die Ruinenstätte und ihre Geschichte.* 5th ed. Vienna: Österreichisches Archäologisches Institut, 1964.

Kleiner, Gerhard. *Die Ruinen von Milet.* Berlin: W. de Gruyter, 1968.

Magie, David. *Roman Rule in Asia Minor.* 2 vols. Princeton: Princeton University Press, 1950.

Meinardus, Otto F. A. "The Christian Remains of the Seven Churches of the Apocalypse." *BA* 37 (1974): 69–82.

_____. *St. John of Patmos and the Seven Churches of the Apocalypse.* Athens: Lycabettus, 1974.

Mellink, M. J. "Archaeology in Asia Minor." *AJA* 78 (1974): 105–30; 79 (1975): 201–22; 80 (1976): 261–90; 81 (1977): 289–322; 82 (1978): 315–38.

Metzger, Henri. *Anatolia II.* London: Cresset, 1969.

Millar, Fergus. *The Emperor in the Roman World.* London: Duckworth, 1977.

Mounce, Robert H. *The Book of Revelation.* Grand Rapids: Wm. B. Eerdmans, 1977.

Page, D. L. *History and the Homeric Iliad.* Berkeley: University of California Press, 1959.

Price, M. J., and Trell, B. L. *Coins and Their Cities.* London: V. C. Vecchi, 1977; Detroit: Wayne State University Press, 1977.

Ramsay, W. M. *The Cities and Bishoprics of Phrygia.* 2 vols. Oxford: Clarendon Press, 1895, 1897.

_____. *Letters to the Seven Churches.* Grand Rapids: Baker, 1979 reprint.

_____. *The Social Basis of Roman Power in Asia Minor.* Amsterdam: A. M. Hakkert, 1967 reprint.

Robert, Louis. *Études Anatoliennes.* Amsterdam: A. M. Hakkert, 1970 reprint of 1937 edition.

_____. *Les Gladiateurs dans l'Orient Grec.* Amsterdam: A. M. Hakkert, 1971 reprint of 1940 edition.

_____. "Sur des inscriptions d'Éphèse." *Revue de Philologie* 41 (1967): 7–84.

Safrai, S., and Stern, M., eds. *The Jewish People in the First Century.* Assen: Van Gorcum, 1974; Philadelphia: Fortress Press, 1974.

Salditt-Trappmann, R. *Tempel der ägyptischen Götter in Griechenland und an der Westküste Kleinasiens.* Leiden: E. J. Brill, 1970.

Sherk, R. K. *Roman Documents from the Greek East.* Baltimore: Johns Hopkins University Press, 1969.

*Studies Presented to George M. A. Hanfmann.* Edited by D. G. Mitten, J. G. Pedley, and J. A. Scott. Mainz: P. von Zabern, 1972.

Trench, R. C. *Commentary on the Epistles to the Seven Churches in Asia.* Minneapolis: Klock and Klock, 1978 reprint of 1897 edition.

Vermeule, C. C. *Roman Imperial Art in Greece and Asia Minor.* Cambridge: Harvard University Press, 1968.

Webster, T. B. L. *Hellenistic Poetry and Art.* New York: Barnes and Noble, 1964.

Wycherley, R. E. *How the Greeks Built Cities.* London: Macmillan, 1962.

Yamauchi, E. M. *Greece and Babylon.* Grand Rapids: Baker, 1967.

_____. *The Stones and the Scriptures.* Philadelphia: J. B. Lippincott, 1972.

Ziegenaus, Oscar, and Luca, Gioia de. *Altertümer von Pergamon: Das Asklepieion.* 2 vols. Berlin: W. de Gruyter, 1968, 1975.

# INDEXES

## I. Index of Subjects

174 **Archaeology in Western Asia Minor**

Sanctuary 108
Saracens 159
Scholastica 100
School 100
Scipio 108
Scipio, Publius Cornelius 51
Seleucids 83, 148
Seleucus I 130
Seljuk Turks 159
Serapeum 83 n.12
Serapis 43, 83 n.12, 126, 143
Severus, Septimius 29, 49, 69, 149, 153
Severus Alexander 52, 67
Silversmith 90
Socrates 95
Stadium 58, 123, 134, 140, 142f.
Strabo 57, 145, 151, 157
Sulla 17
Swimming pool 90, 123 n.17
Synagogue 69, 125f.

Tacitus 57, 140
Taurobolium 45 n.45
Temple 69, 126, 150
Tertullian 78
Textiles 53

Thales 118
Theater 38, 94, 123, 143, 149, 152
Theodosius 110 n.100
Tiberius 57, 67, 90, 119, 139
Titus 58, 140, 142
Tombs 153, 160
Trajan 42f., 58, 86, 119, 123, 129f., 140, 161
Trajanus, Marcus Ulpius 86, 140
Trophimus 118
Tübingen School 18
Turks 15, 87
Tyche 57, 102, 143

Valerian 104
Vedius, Antoninus 86, 90
Venatio 92
Verulanus, Claudius 90
Verus, Lucius 67
Vespasian 85, 91, 140, 142
Vesta 88
Vitruvius 35 n.11

Xenophon 157
Xerxes 157

Zeus 58, 69, 78, 134, 143, 145

## II. Index of Places

Actium 118
Adramyttium Gulf 21
Aeolis 55
Akhisar 51f.
Alashehir 77
Alexandria 49, 79
Alexandria Troas 21f.
Anatolia 15
Antioch 60, 79
Apamea 137
Aphrodisias 125
Ardabav 78
Asia 15–17, 21, 109
Asia Minor 15
Assos 21–29
Athens 48, 93

Bayrakli 56
Berlin 122
Bithynia 22

Caesarea 106
Caicus River 31
Cayster River 79
Cilicia 137, 151
Claros 145, 151
Colossae 53, 155–61
Constantinople 15, 25
Corinth 49, 94

Delphi 130, 134
Denizli 135, 141

## III. Index of Authors and Excavators

Ramage, N. H. 68 n.21
Ramsay, W. M. 18–19; 31 n.2;
  41 n.29; 42 n.33; 54 n.18; 58
  n.11; 61 n.21; 62 n.24; 68
  n.23; 77; 81 n.2; 93 n.41;
  106; 109 nn.92, 95; 110
  n.96; 113 n.107; 137 nn.2,
  3; 142 n.16; 143 n.17; 145
  n.26; 151 n.10; 152 n.14;
  154 n.23; 159 nn.4, 5; 163
  n.1; 165 n.7
Rayet, O. 131
Real, W. 120 n.10, 127 n.29
Reinhold, M. 54 nn.15, 19
Robert, L. 71 n.32; 86 n.23; 91
  nn.33, 35; 93 n.43; 94 n.46;
  95 n.50; 100 n.64; 109 n.93;
  142 nn.15, 16; 143 nn.19,
  22; 145 nn.23–25, 27; 153
  nn.17, 18; 161 n.14
Rödel, V. 127 n.29
Roth-Gerson, L. 71 n.31
Rudwick, M. J. S. 141 n.11

Safrai, S. 53 n.12, 71 n.32, 110
  n.99, 152 n.14
Salditt-Trappmann, R. 43
  n.43, 83 n.12, 126 n.27
Schatzman, P. 34
Schliemann, H. 21
Schoedel, W. R. 61 n.16
Scott, J. A. 74 n.39, 119 n.6
Scramuzza, V. M. 67 n.18
Scranton, R. 26 n.15
Seager, A. R. 71 n.34
Shepherd, M. A. 60 n.15
Sherk, R. K. 51 n.2, 66, 67
  n.15, 92 n.36, 139 n.5
Sherwin-White, A. N. 16 n.8,
  81 n.3
Skilton, J. 19 n.20
Smallwood, E. M. 17 n.12

Soedel, C. W. 26 n.16
Sokolowski, F. 107 n.87
Spalinger, A. J. 65 n.2
Starr, C. G. 16 n.7
Stern, M. 53 n.12, 71 n.32, 110
  n.99, 152 n.14
Strocka, V. M. 88, 97 n.51, 98
  n.52, 99 n.59, 100 n.62

Tarn, W. 35 n.11
Taylor, L. R. 109 n.95
Tcherikover, V. 149
Thomas, A. 131
Thompson, H. A. 33 n.6
Toynbee, J. M. C. 92 n.38
Trell, B. L. 104 n.77, 106
  n.83; *see also as coauthor with*
  Price, M. J.
Trench, R. C. 51 n.1, 77, 78
  n.3, 87 n.25, 137 n.2
Triomphe, R. 36 n.19
Tuchelt, K. 122 n.16, 129, 131

Ueblacker, M. 127 n.29

Vermaseren, M. J. 45 n.45, 69
  n.24
Vermeule, C. C. 28 nn.22–25;
  42 n.36; 52 nn. 6, 7; 58 nn.7,
  8; 59 n.12; 60 n.14; 66 n.13;
  67 nn.18, 19; 78 n.5; 83
  nn.10, 13; 84 n.14; 86 n.19;
  90 n.28; 119 n.7; 140 n.7;
  143 n.21; 149 n.5; 161 n.12
Verzone, P. 149, 153 n.15, 154
  n.22
Vetters, H. 88, 97 n.51, 99,
  100 n.65, 102 n.73, 111
  n.105
Ville, V. G. 94 n.48
Voigtländer, W. 132 n.8

Wagner, G. 45 n.45
Waldbaum, J. C. 65 n.5, 69 n.24, 77 n.1
Walker, D. 68 n.20
Webster, T. B. L. 36 n.16, 98 n.53
Weickert, C. 120
Wiegand, T. 120, 131
Wilberg, W. 99 n.59
Wilkinson, L. P. 139 n.4
Winger, F. E. 26 n.15
Wiseman, D. J. 66 n.11
Wood, J. 87
Woodhead, A. G. 17 n.12, 52 n.4

Wotschitzky, A. 106 n.84
Wright, D. F. 78 n.8
Wycherley, R. E. 26 n.18, 33 n.6, 39 n.24, 122 n.15

Yamauchi, E. M. 16 n.4, 18 n.17, 19 n.20, 21 n.2, 39 n.25, 43 n.39, 45 n.45, 65 n.3, 157 n.2
Yegül, F. K. 39 n.24
Young, W. J. 65 n.7

Ziegenaus, O. 34 n.9, 45 n.48, 48 n.49

## IV. Index of Scriptures

**Acts**
13:16   125
13:26   125
13:43   125
16:6–8   22
16:8   21
16:9   22
16:11   21
16:14   53
17:4   125
17:17   125
17:28   24, 98 n.54
19   81
19:9   99f.
19:10   15, 157
19:23ff.   94f.
19:32ff.   81
19:40ff.   81
20:5–6   21
20:6   22
20:13–14   22, 29
20:15–17   118
20:31   81
20:38   22

21:8–9   154
21:39   165
27:2   15

**1 Corinthians**
15:32   92
15:33   98

**2 Corinthians**
2:12   21
9:1–4   165

**Colossians**
1:4   157
1:7   157
2:1   135, 157
4:9   157
4:12–13   157
4:13   135, 147
4:15–16   135

**2 Timothy**
4:13   21
4:20   118

**Titus**
1:12   98 n.54

**Philemon**
10–12   157

**Revelation**
1:11   32, 51, 55, 63, 77, 81, 135
1:15   53
2:1   81
2:8   55
2:9   61
2:13   32
2:18   51, 53
2:24   51
3:1   63
3:4   63
3:7   77
3:14   135
3:16   141
3:17   140
3:18   146